"HOT STUFF!"
Firefighting Collectibles
An Illustrated Reference and Buyers Guide

NEWLY REVISED AND EXPANDED

by
Andrew G. Gurka

© Copyright 1994
Andrew G. Gurka

3rd Printing 2001

Published by:
L-W Book Sales
P.O. Box 69
Gas City, IN 46933

LAD -
USE 3

Dedication

This book is dedicated to the members of the fire service, past and present, who have accepted risks and have vowed to serve and protect others.

Acknowledgments

Special thanks to the following individuals for contributing photos and information:

Paul Klaver - 5 Viking Ct. #43, Arlington, MA, 02174
Ken Sodderbeck
Jerry Pajak
Philip Halstead
Charlie Kehoe
Edward Vasko
Warren Lun
Sidney A. Alpert, Communication & Technology Collection,
        12514 Davan, Silver Spring, MD 20904
Glenn Robinson
Glenn Hartley, Sr.
Richard Bosanko
Gary Carino
Tom D'Arcangelo
Steve Harris
Jacques Noel Jacobsen Jr.
Steve Jimmerson
Mike Kulklinski
Arnold Merkitch
Terry Sullivan
Dave Miller
Jim Roan, Reference Librarian, National Museum of
        American History, Library, Smithsonian Institution

Preface

Journey together with collector Andrew Gurka through the fascinating world of firefighting collectibles.

Explore rare 19th Century catalogs and curious illustrations of firefighting equipment.

View over 300 photographs of firefighting collectibles, including a special color section on fire grenades and hats & helmets.

Discover current values and helpful tips on acquiring firefighting collectibles.

Delve into the noble history of firefighting and ponder the old ways of the fire laddies.

Table of Contents

About the Author

Andrew Gurka is a certified, full time Fire Inspector and Paramedic for the City of Dearborn Heights, Michigan. Mr. Gurka possesses a Bachelor's of Science Degree in Occupational Safety & Health and a Master's of Science Degree in Business. Mr. Gurka has a passion for Firefighting Collectibles and wishes to share his knowledge with fellow enthusiasts.

His interest in firefighting collectibles began with his career in the fire department. As a boy, he played with toy fire trucks and visited the local fire station. The firemen were very friendly and he enjoyed looking around the station. After graduating from college, he took a desk job with an insurance company. Every time he heard the siren of a fire truck or rescue squad, he felt he should be riding with the firefighters. He made up his mind to quit his job and train to become a firefighter. One year later he was hired and sent to the fire academy. As he learned the techniques and tools of modern firefighting, he wondered how difficult firefighting must have been 100 years ago. Old firefighting equipment and memorabilia seemed very interesting and offered insight about the past.

The first item he acquired was an old fire extinquisher for $5.00 from a salvage yard. Wherever he went, be it a flea market or antique store, he would inquire about firefighting collectibles. Many times the vendor or store owner would reply: "Fire stuff - don't have enough of it." or "that stuff always sells quickly." He soon realized firefighting collectibles were "hot stuff" and has been adding to his collection ever since.

To truly understand firefighting collectibles, one must draw from many other areas of collecting. The novice and advanced collector alike will constantly be challenged with locating and learning about these items. Although many firefighting collectibles are quite valuable and make good investments, the most important rule of collecting is to have fun.

By the way, he still likes playing with fire trucks. Stop by the station some time and he will show you around.

Mr. Gurka enjoys discussing firefighting collectibles and is always interested in buying, selling, and trading, to upgrade his collection. Andrew also specializes in the restoration of firefighting collectibles and antiques.

You may contact him at: Fireman's Roost
Andrew G. Gurka
37930 Birch Run
Livonia, MI 48150

Introduction

One may ask "What is so fascinating about firefighting collectibles?"

Maybe it's not so much what the items are, but rather what these items represent. Surrounding firefighting collectibles is the aura of a full range of human experiences and emotions.

Within these firefighting collectibles exists the pride in being a firefighter, in serving others, and keeping old traditions alive.

The excitement of the alarm, the anxiety of the unknown, and the hope everything will work out, can be felt.

The clanging bells, the screaming siren, the roar of the engine can be heard.

The sparkling fire engine, the brightly flashing red lights, the men in helmets and fire coats can be envisioned.

Feel the camaraderie of the firefighters.
Marvel at the accomplishments of teamwork and the skill and heroism of the individual.

The smell of smoke is in the air. Deadly, black smoke.

Near are the intense, searing flames.

Open the nozzle and feel the vibrations of cool water rushing to extinguish the blaze.

Know the immense sadness of loss and appreciate the gratitude of those helped.

Laugh with friends in the sheer joy of celebration and engage in the spirit of competition.

Yes it's all here, the danger, triumphs, and heartbreaks of firefighting. Welcome, explore the discoveries, inventions and lessons of the past. Begin to get a better understanding of the present and fuel ideas for the future.

The intent of this book is to show a wide range of firefighting collectibles, to indicate approximate values of these items, to reveal helpful tips on purchasing firefighting collectibles, to provide illustrations and descriptions from old fire supply catalogs, and to offer the reader a modicum of history pertaining to each item. This book does not attempt to show or describe, every possible firefighting collectible ever made.

General Guidelines for Purchasing Fire Collectibles

Caveat Emptor - "Let the buyer beware"
Most collectibles don't have a warranty, therefore the buyer takes the risk of quality and authenticity upon himself.

Always try to find a complete item without any missing, damaged, or modified parts.

It is better to pass on purchasing a substandard item. Eventually the item you seek will appear, probably in far better condition than the previous item.

An item in excellent, original condition is preferable to a restored item.

Generally, the demand, condition, age, and availability of an item are the prime factors determining value.

Demand for an item is the most important element of price.

Unusual or elaborate designs and fine workmanship can greatly increase the value of an item.

Just because an item sold at an auction or was seen in a book at a certain price, doesn't guarantee an item is worth that amount. An item is only worth what the buyer will pay at that point in time.

Beware of items that look "too new". They probably are. Many fire collectibles have been or are being reproduced. Examples include cast iron fire toys, leather fire buckets, trumpets, posters, prints, signs and shaving mugs.

Reproductions are prolific, yet some reproduced items are now scarce and still desirable for display purposes. For example, many collectors would rather purchase a reproduced cast iron fire engine for $50, than spend $1200 or more for an original.

Many fire collectibles are being sought by folk art collectors and fire apparatus restorers.

Learn where an item came from and how to contact the seller.

If there is ever any doubt as to the authenticity of an item, consult a reputable collector or antique dealer that specializes in fire collectibles.

A Note Regarding Prices

The prices listed in this book are not fixed values and should serve the collector as a guide only. Prices listed in this volume are based on data gathered from collectors, auction catalogs, swap meets, internet, and mail order houses. This information can reflect the trends of buying and selling in the firefighting collectibles market. The collector should be aware that rare and unusual items that can be attributed to famous individuals may be bid to unpredictably high prices at auction. Neither the author nor the publisher can be held responsible for gains or losses from using this price guide.

Where Does One Go to Find Firefighting Collectibles?

Fire department swap meets.

Fire conventions and expositions.

Mail order houses that sell firefighting collectibles.

Local and national collectors.

Antique dealers.

Flea markets.

Estate sales.

Garage sales.

Auctions.

Internet Auctions & Ads

Surplus or obsolete items from cities or towns.

Trade-in items found at fire apparatus dealers or fire equipment supply houses.

Run want ad.

What Happens at a Firefighting Collectibles Swap Meet?

You will look at everything at least a half a dozen times.

You will see things you can't afford.

You will bump into an old friend.

You will meet a new friend.

You will decide not to buy a particular item. Later on, you'll regret not purchasing the item.

You will wish your wallet had another "twenty" in it.

You will have fun.

You will be hooked.

Tip: Have you ever attended a swap meet right when it opened, yet noticed that most of the premium items were already gone?

Many dealers and vendors buy, sell and trade with each other before the swap meet opens to the public. Consider buying dealer space and gathering up a few items to sell. That way, you'll get the best selection of firefighting collectibles.

Tip: Always barter to receive the best price. Try a low offer and if it is not accepted, ask: What's the lowest you'll go on this item? Sometimes you may be surprised at the low price the seller will volunteer.

Auctions (Helpful Hints)

Be sure to arrive early and thoroughly inspect the items you are interested in bidding on.

Assure that the item or items you will be bidding on haven't been damaged during the preview.

Find out if there is a reserve on any particular items.

Obtain a bidder number and position yourself so you can see the auctioneer.

When placing a bid, be sure you know exactly what you are bidding on and the value of the bid.

Auctions can be very exciting. Try not to get caught up in bidding war. Set the highest price that you are willing to pay for an item in your mind and stick to it.

An auction with hundreds of items can last quite a long time. This necessitates waiting for certain items you may be interested in bidding on. On many occasions, if a collector expresses interest in a particular item to an auction worker, the item may be expedited to the auction block.

Auction Tips

Be assertive. If you try to bid so nobody else can see, chances are the auctioneer won't see you either. The aggressive bidder will claim the item, while the timid bidder will go home empty handed.

It it's one item you seek, be careful you are not bidding on a group of items that you may not want or can afford.

After the item is yours, gather it up promptly. If its too large or heavy to remove immediately, tag the item sold with your name.

It is not uncommon to be required to apply for a bidding number. You will be asked to show some identification such as a valid driver's license.

If you successfully bid on an item, and find a hidden flaw or problem that would have affected your purchase of the item, call attention to it immediately. Don't wait until the auction is over to resolve the situation.

Any item that is claimed to be genuine and is not, may be returned to the auction house for a refund. That is your right as upheld by the law.

Number Rating System (1-5)
Condition of Firefighting Collectibles

1 - Premium condition, appears almost as new, showing virtually no wear, extremely well preserved.

2 - Excellent condition, complete with only slight wear, showing normal aging.

3 - Average condition, showing standard wear and repair, slight deterioration.

4 - Below average condition, some damage and missing parts, moderate deterioration.

5 - Extremely poor condition, improperly cared for, severely deteriorated.

Collectors should make every attempt to buy an item in the best condition they can afford. At a later time, it may be possible to sell or trade the item for one in better condition.

Firefighting typically puts a tremendous amount of wear and tear on equipment in addition to the normal aging process. It may be difficult to find many collectibles in #1 condition. Therefore, the prices in this book reflect items in #2 condition unless otherwise noted.

Unless extremely rare or unusual, items in #5 condition are usually one step from the junkyard and should be avoided.

Advertising Giveaways, Premiums & Related Items

In the late 1800's, many businesses would offer customers useful items for free, to encourage a customer's trade. If the item was a giveaway, there was no charge and no requirement for purchase. A premium, on the other hand, usually required some type of purchase.

Insurance companies, fire apparatus builders, fire equipment supply makers, breweries, tobacco companies and many others, produced advertising giveaways and premiums that are related to firefighting. Items of this nature have become quite collectible. In addition, there is a group of collectors devoted entirely to gathering insurance company advertising items.

Giveaways and premiums encompass a full spectrum of useful items and trifles. Items include: calendars, ashtrays, matchsafes, inkwells, blotters, paperweights, pens, rulers, letter openers, bottle openers, mirrors, tokens, cards and pin-back buttons.

Many other items were given away as salesmen's samples. These items were miniature examples of the actual product. Salesmen's samples of leather helmets, fire hydrants, fire buckets, boots and wood ladders are very desirable.

Matchsafes and inkwells are in high demand, especially unusual or finely crafted examples. Old calendars with color illustrations of fire apparatus are much more common. A collector may want to specialize, given the large variety of items available.

Complete set of six Comical Trade Cards,
"The Firemen", circa 1880's.

Advertising Giveaways, Premiums & Related Items

Left - Action in Jackson Beer six pack.
Right - Harlan Gold Beer.

Tokiem Gas Pump w/
Texaco Fire Chief
Gasoline Advertising,
1955.

Silver Spring Brewery Advertisement.

Pabst Blue Ribbon Beer Advertising Print.

Advertising Giveaways, Premiums & Related Items

Post Cereal Premiums, Mickey the Fire Chief,
Card Board Cutouts, Circa 1930's.

Texaco Fire Chief,
Gasoline Advertisement, 1950

Inkwell, Fire Association of Philadelphia, in
the shape of an early hydrant.

Advertisement for 1956 Chevrolet.

Advertising Giveaways, Premiums & Related Items

Smoking Related Collectibles.

Pair of Ashtrays, Grinnell Sprinkler Head.

Matchholder and Ashtray,
Eureka Fire Hose.

Player Cigarette Cards, set of 50.

Aetna Insurance Co. Calendar,
with horse drawn steamer,
dated 1897.

Miniature Pair of
Candee Fire Boots,
Salesmen's Sample,
3" Tall.

Gamewell Advertising Mirror.

Advertising Giveaways, Premiums & Related Items

PRICE GUIDE FOR ADVERTISING GIVEAWAYS, PREMIUMS & RELATED ITEMS

Aetna Insurance Co. Calendar 1897 – $175
Ash tray - Eureka fire hose - $67.50
Ash tray - Gamewell Fire Alarm - $67.50
Ash tray - Grinnell sprinkler head - $65.00
Beer Advertising - Pabst Good Old Time Flavor - $30.00
Beer Advertising - Silver Spring Brewery - $100.00
Beer can - Harlan Gold - $5.50
Beer cans - Action in Jackson beer, 6 pk - $25.00
Blotter - Firemen's Fund Insurance Co. - $27.50
Blotter - Hartford Fire Insurance Co. - $25.00
Bottle opener - marked Seagrave - $25.00
Calendar - American La France, 1950's - $65.00
Cigar box - Welcome Fireman, wood, 1931 - $30.00
Clock - Fireman's Insurance Co. - $1100.00
Coffee Tin - Fire Fighters Signature Blend, made for Memphis,TN Fire Dept. - $18.00
Gamewell Advertising Mirror – $250
Gas Pump - Tokiem w/Fire Chief advertising, 1955 - $2350.00
Inkwell - Fire Assoc. of Philadelphia - $350.00
Knife - Franklin Fire Insurance - $45.00
Magazine ad - Texaco Fire Chief gasoline - $12.50
Magazine ad - 1956 Chevrolet - $12.50
Matchbook - Fire Chief gasoline - $12.50
Matcholder - Eureka Fire Hose, brass - $55.00
Matchsafe - Home Ins. Co., sterling silver w/horse drawn steamer - $500.00
Matchsafe - Home Ins. Co., sterling silver w/fireman - $600.00
Mirror - 4" diameter, Fire & Marine Insurane Co. - $50.00
Paperweight - glass w/photo of horse drawn fire wagon - $80.00
Pin - Pennsylvania State Fireman's Association, 1911 - $22.50
Pin - Pep cereal, Smokey Stover (1946) - $22.50
Pin - Pep cereal, The Chief (1945) - $22.50
Pocketknife - Home Insurance Company - $75.00
Ruler - Fireman's Fund Insurance, wood - $12.00
Trade cards - "The Firemen" set of six, Cosak & Clarke - $175.00
Trade cards - Player cigarettes, set of 50 - $125.00
Tub Tobacco - unopened - $75.00
Tip Top Tobacco - unopened - $85.00

Salesmen's samples.
Fire boots - pair of "Candee" - $95.00
Fire boots - pair of Goodyear Mfg. Co. - $75.00
Leather fire bucket - $325.00
Red Comet sample kit - $180.00
Miniature leather helmet front (modern) - $32.50
Working model of fire hydrant - $600.00

Cereal Premium, Post, Mickey the Fire Chief, cardboard, 1930's - $85.00

Alarm Apparatus for Firehouses

Firehouse gongs.

When a fire alarm box is actuated, the signal is transmitted to a central station. At the central station, secondary circuits transmit the alarm to the proper firehouse gong.

Firehouse gongs have electro-mechanisms designed to strike a bell. Gong mechanisms were usually mounted in a wood case. Many gongs had beautiful oak, mahogany, or walnut cases with a polished brass bell. The door on a gong has a glass panel through which the mechanism is visible.

Gongs were available in bell sizes 6, 8, 10, 12, 15 and 18 inches in diameter. If a gong was to be installed outside, it could be ordered in a weatherproof case.

Generally, the larger the gong, the more valuable. Firehouse gongs with handsome wood cases in excellent condition, are highly sought after. Unlike other firefighting equipment, each firehouse only had one gong. This fact makes firehouse gongs one of the best investments of all firefighting collectibles.

Turtle gongs.

Gongs of this type have the striking hammer mounted on the inside of the bell. These gongs were designed to be dust and moisture resistant and were made in 6 or 10 inch diameter sizes. Turtle gongs, while collectible, are not as valuable as firehouse gongs with wood cases.

Tappers.

Tappers were alarm devices equipped with small bells 4 to 6 inches in diameter. These bells were usually mounted on desk tops at station headquarters or firehouses. They were electrically operated and made in a numbers of styles.

Visual indicators.

Indicators were spring driven, electro-mechanical devices which would show the number of a fire alarm box that was actuated. These devices could indicate numbers of boxes 1 to 999 or 1 to 9999 for larger cities. The actual workings of the indicator were mounted in a finely crafted wood case. Some indicators had a continuous ringing bell placed above the case as a part of the unit. Other indicators were mounted with an electro-mechanical gong below the indicator. Devices of this nature were known as indicating gongs. Indicating gongs are the most desirable items of firehouse alarm apparatus. A large indicating gong with a finely crafted oak case, would be one of the showpieces of virtually any collection.

Registers & Timestamps.

A register was a device that would punch holes in a paper tape. The number of holes punched in the tape would correspond to the fire alarm box that was actuated. As the paper tape passed through the time stamp, the exact time was printed on the tape. After the tape passed through the register and time stamp, it was wound on a take up reel. The tape gave firemen a permanent record of all alarms received at the firehouse.

Engine house clocks.

Many firehouses had a special clock that did more than merely show time. One version of an engine house clock had two dials. One dial showed continuous time, while the other dial was electrically stopped when a fire alarm was received. The Umbria clock was another type of engine house clock. This clock was used to test the fire alarm system.

Alarm Apparatus for Firehouses

ELECTRO MECHANICAL GONG.

(W. SMITH'S PATENT.)

May be used
on either
an open or
closed
circuit.

Recovers so
quickly
that it can be
used in
connection
with
the quickest
District
Call Box.

Will
not miss or
strike a
double blow.

As the
blows are
struck
by a gravity
escapement,
needs
winding but
once
for each 300
blows.

FIG. 160.

WALNUT OR OAK CASES.   MAHOGANY, WHEN SO ORDERED.

7-inch Gong............	14-inch Gong............
8-inch Gong............	16-inch Gong............
10-inch Gong............	18-inch Gong............
12-inch Gong............	20-inch Gong............

Alarm Apparatus for Firehouses

**VISUAL INDICATORS COMBINED WITH
ELECTRO-MECHANICAL GONGS**

Where both visual and audible signals are desired the combination of our visual indicator and electro-mechanical single stroke gong presents an effective arrangement for accomplishing this result.

The mechanisms of the two instruments while installed in the same case are entirely separate and distinct, each acting as a check on the other.

Indicators may be combined, as shown in the accompanying illustrations, with the 8-inch, 12-inch, 15-inch and 18-inch gongs.

No. 306

No. 310

EIGHT-INCH ELECTRO-MECHANICAL GONG
Combined with Visual indicator

MUNICIPAL FIRE ALARM SYSTEMS

DIRECT ACTING TAPPER WITH SIX-INCH GONG

GAMEWELL TURTLE GONG

No. 305

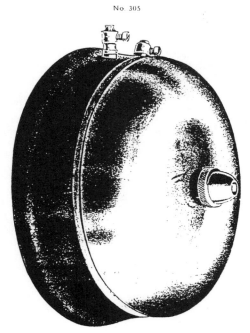

DUST AND MOISTURE are the greatest enemies of the ordinary fire alarm gong. In designing this gong special attention has been paid to protect it thoroughly against moisture, dust, and other conditions which would cause deterioration. All of the moving parts of the mechanism, except the hammer, are snugly inclosed in a cover beneath the bell. The joint between the cover and the case is carefully machined flat and true to make it dust and insect proof, and the cover is fastened down tightly with three screws. The operating parts of the mechanism are mounted independent of the cover so that the cover can be readily removed for inspection without disabling the mechanism.

The bell is of the highest grade of bell metal, 10 in. in diameter, and gives a pure, clear tone. It is turned and finished on the outside and held in place by a fancy acorn top bronze nut. It is arranged to strike correctly all signals which come in over the circuit, and when properly adjusted and in good working condition will not miss blows or give double blows. This gong is electro-mechanical in operation and will strike two hundred and fifty blows on one winding.

Two sets of terminals are provided, one outside the case and one inside, to make it easy to mount the gong over a conduit box or other receptacle.

The turtle gong is an important part of the fire alarm system. It must be designed to work with the rest of your apparatus and it must not fail. Our sixty years of experience is a guarantee that this gong can always be depended upon.

SALES SPECIFICATIONS

The gong shall be made as outlined above. It shall be capable of operating at the rate of two blows a second and have a capacity of two hundred and fifty blows at one winding. The bell shall be of the best grade of bell metal, 10 in. in diameter. Two sets of terminals shall be provided. The electrically operated parts shall require but a minimum of current and shall work properly with all ordinary variations in the current. With the exception of the armature spring, all parts shall be permanently fitted and shall need no adjustment in operation. The shaftings shall be of steel and the main wheel, hammer, levers, etc., shall be of Excelsior bronze.

GAMEWELL ELECTRO-MECHANICAL TURTLE GONG
Gongs of this design are made with bells 6" and 10" in diameter

The Gamewell Company
NEWTON UPPER FALLS, MASS.

Alarm Apparatus for Firehouses

GAMEWELL DIAPHONES
(Compressed Air)

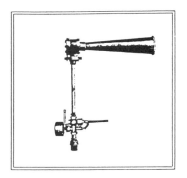

A FIRE ALARM THAT REALLY SAYS FIRE

The Gamewell Company
NEWTON UPPER FALLS, MASS.

Peerless Take-up Reel
A new reel with distinct improvements

THIS NEW TAKE-UP REEL has four advantages over the ordinary older style reel. Regardless of the [siz]e of the roll of paper the reel maintains [un]iform speed, keeping the paper taut [al]l times. Less winding is necessary, [tw]o windings will do the work that re[quir]ed six or eight windings on the older [reel]. The train work is completely en[close]d in a dustproof case, protecting the [mech]anism and insuring longer service. [Spe]cial device has been provided so that [the] reel will be automatically stopped if [p]aper breaks. Arrangements are made

so that the paper can be pulled backwards to inspect previous signals. Winding the reel while it is in service will not interfere in the slightest with its operation. The reel will take any width paper from ½ inch to 2 inch.

The paper wheel and the brake arm are of composition bronze and highly finished. The train work is enclosed in an attractive black lacquered cast-iron case. This new reel is a distinct advance over all previous reels and is guaranteed to give most satisfactory service.

The Gamewell Company
NEWTON UPPER FALLS, MASS.

BOX LINE RECORDING SET

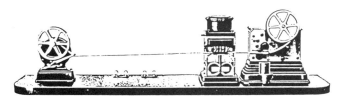

Consisting of Punch Register, Time Stamp with Clock, Peerless Take-up Reel, and Shelf with Brackets and Line Terminals

Punch register with take-up reel

The Gamewell Company
NEWTON UPPER FALLS, MASS.

Ideal Punch Register

THIS register provides a permanent visual record of any signals which may pass over a fire alarm circuit by punching holes one-eighth inch in diameter in a paper tape. The tape, one-half inch wide, runs outside of the instrument to prevent paper fuzz from getting into the operating mechanism. A removable cup is provided to catch all punchings.

The register is usually mounted on a shelf, and continuity springs are provided so that the register may be removed without the necessity for disconnecting wires. If the register is to be mounted

on slate or marble a different size of continuity spring will be provided.

The base and cup for clippings are black lacquered. The side plates are of Excelsior bronze with bevelled plate glass in the top and ends. This glass is removable to permit ready inspection and easy access. These registers are used not only in fire headquarters and apparatus houses but also in industrial concerns and the offices of the waterworks, electric, gas and street railroad companies.

The Gamewell Company
NEWTON UPPER FALLS, MASS.

Alarm Apparatus for Firehouses

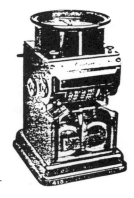

Excelsior Time and Date Stamp

An accurate record of the time that all alarms are received is a real necessity in an up-to-date fire alarm system. The Excelsior Time Stamp automatically stamps the minute, hour, day, month, and year on the edge of the register paper immediately after the signal has been recorded. It is supplied with a clock as shown above or connected with a master clock when more than one time stamp is used. The date stamp should be wound once a day, and after it has been once started it takes care of long months, short months, and leap year days and century days without manual shifting of dates.

The minute wheel on the date stamp is electrically connected with the clock and is moved forward once each minute. This operates the hour, day, and month wheels in turn. Register paper may be inserted or removed without mutilating the paper even though the stamp is set up. This stamp is ten and a quarter inches high, with special Excelsior Bronze side plates and beveled plate glass to permit ready inspection of the mechanism. It is provided with terminal contacts and continuity springs for ease in installation and removal. The number wheels are of hard rolled brass, and it is built throughout with all the care of fine watchmaking.

AUTOMATIC WHISTLE BLOWING MACHINE

This Whistle Blowing Machine can be used to operate a Compressed Air Signal, or a steam whistle where there is a pressure of 80 lbs. of steam day and night, holidays and Sundays. It makes possible crisp, clear blasts, properly spaced and accurately timed. The contact magnets are connected directly with the fire alarm circuit.

The operating mechanism can be located in a tower, on a roof, or any place where a sufficient drop can be provided for the weights. It is desirable that space be provided for a fifty-foot drop wherever possible, although perfectly satisfactory results are obtained with less drop.

SALES SPECIFICATIONS
Apparatus:

The apparatus shall consist of a Weight Driven Mechanism to operate valve, necessary chains, weights, pulleys, etc. The driving mechanism shall be electro-mechanical in operation and shall be capable of blowing on the whistle the signal number of any station in the system. It shall be provided with devices for positively timing the length of the blasts, and shall open the whistle valve simultaneously with the breaking of the fire alarm circuit. It shall be provided with necessary chain, weights, weight rods, and pulley so installed as not to interfere with the use of the whistle for other purposes. Shall be provided with winding devices readily operative by one person. Shall be provided with plug switch lightning arrester so that the machine can be cut out for repairs or testing.

Steam Gong and Balance Valve shown in upper part of illustration not included unless specified

Excelsior Punch Register

This register is used to furnish a permanent record of alarms received i offices, engine houses, and elsewhere, where a single circuit register is req punches a sharp, clear-cut hole one-quarter inch in diameter on the tape, a plied with a removable cup to catch all cuttings. The tape runs complete the mechanism, where it will not carry lint or dust into the operating parts. A device automatically stops the feeding of the paper after the signal is comp a sufficient length of blank paper run to clearly differentiate the signals. T can be adjusted for use with or without a time stamp.

It can be arranged for closed or open circuit and can be equipped with tir gong and other local contacts. The controlling magnets are mounted in the are readily accessible and removable without disturbing the operating me It is equipped with continuity springs for easy electrical connection. The end of the register are of heavy beveled plate glass, so that the condition of the m can be readily determined at any time. The side plates and frame work are o bronze, the shafting, pinions, locking and tripping levers of the best grade of st paper reel carries a one-inch register tape, and is so arranged that the registe can be easily replaced. This register is built in a sturdy, substantial manner l skilled workmen and of the best materials.

Indicator Combined

WITH

GONG STRIKER.

This instrument represented as per cut consists of an indicator combined with the different sizes of Gongs, each with its own magnet and acting entirely independent of each other, so that if the gongs should accidentally miss a blow, the indicator will not fail to make the right record.

Price complete. . . . .

FIG. 161.

"CROW FOOT" GRAVITY BATTERY.

FIG. 161.

Sizes.	Main 5 x 7 inches.	Local. 6 x 8 inches.
Cell, complete.		. . . .
Jar.		. . . .
Zinc, with Connector . .		. . . .
Copper		. . . .

The Gamewell Company
NEWTON UPPER FALLS, MASS.

Original Catalog Pages

Alarm Apparatus for Firehouses

6" TORONTO TAPPER

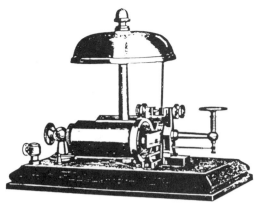

UPRIGHT CALL BELL

A COMPACT electrically operated, direct action, single stroke bell unit for audibly announcing signals. It is especially adapted for use in fire headquarters, apparatus houses, industrial concerns, offices of the water works, electric. gas and street railway companies. The size is 7½ inches high over all, 9½ inches long, 5¼ inches wide, and 1 inch thick at the base.

The bell is of the best quality bell metal, 4½ inches in diameter, arranged to be fastened in either of two positions near the center of the base to allow for either closed or open circuit operatie

The operating magnets are enclosed in bronz black lacquered tubing and supported on the ba so as to allow adjusting for length of air gap. A justable front and back stop screws mounted the base beside the armature lever limit the arm ture travel.

The majority of metal parts are of cast comp sition bronze of hand-grained finish, heavily coat with lacquer. The entire unit is mounted on polished oak base.

The Gamewell Company
NEWTON UPPER FALLS, MASS.

The Gamewell Company
NEWTON UPPER FALLS, MASS.

UMBRIA CLOCK

Umbria Clock with Electrical Contacts
for Testing Fire Alarm System

ENGINE HOUSE TRIPS.

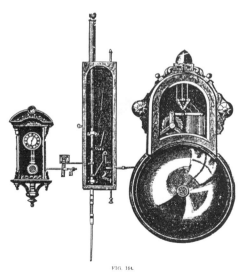

FIG. 164.

The Engine House Trip is used in connection with Electric Fire Alarm System, for the purpose of shortening the time required to make ready to leave the house after an alarm comes in. The trip is placed alongside the alarm bell and by the first backward motion of the hammer of the gong preparatory to striking, the automatic trip lever is freed, which throws the stall doors open, also stopping the clock at the same instant, showing the exact time the alarm comes in. The whole connection is made by simply pulling down the lever at the lower end of the case. It can be arranged to light the gas if desired. It is simple in construction and not likely to get out of order. The above cut represents the trip set in connection with clock and gong.

Used by the leading Fire Departments.

Engine House Trip ....

The Gamewell Company
NEWTON UPPER FALLS, MASS.

Alarm Apparatus for Firehouses

FIG. 55.

One-Quarter Size Cut of 12 inch.
(PATENT APPLIED FOR.)

The above cut represents a portion of the Bell broken away to show the mechanism. These Trip Gongs are especially adapted for use wherever a Signal Bell is needed. They pull from the centre, and the mechanism, which is the most simple of any Trip Gong heretofore made, (and will be very durable) is all concealed under the bell, a new feature in large Gongs of this class. Gongs 10 inches in diameter and upwards furnished with lignumvitae wood hammers.

Polished Bell Metal Gem Trip Gongs.

7 inch, each,...
8 in., " ....

Signal Trip Gongs.

10 inch, Lignumvitae Hammer, each,..
12 inch, " ....

Signal Trip Gongs, Extra Large Sizes.

14 inch, each ....
16 inch, " ....
18 inch, " ....

GONGS.

FIG. 53.

BELL METAL GONGS WITH STRIKING APPARATUS.

This cut shows gong arranged with foot striker. We arrange them also to be struck by a cord, or automatic to be struck by pin in wheels.

	rough,	finished,	nickel plated.
No. 1, 8-inch bell, with striker,			
No. 2, 10 " " "			
No. 3, 12 " " "			
No. 4, 14 " " "			
No. 5, 16 " " "			
No. 6, 18 " " "			
No. 7, 21 " " "			

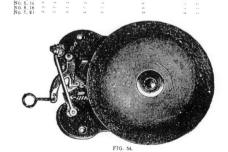

FIG. 54.

BELL METAL ENGINE HOUSE GONGS.

No. 1,	3-inch, finished, bell metal, each............
No. 2,	4 " " " " " ....
No. 3,	5 " " " " " ....
No. 4,	6 " " " " " ....
No. 5,	7 " " " " " ....
No. 6,	8 " " " " " ....
No. 7,	10 " " " " " ....
No. 8,	12 " " " " " ....
No. 9,	14 " " " " " ....
No. 10,	16 " " " " " ....
No. 11,	18 " " " " " ....

INDICATOR.

3 6 5

Alarm Apparatus for Firehouses

10" Gamewell Turtle Gong.

10" Brass Engine House Gong.

12" Fire Alarm Bell - manually rung &
mounted on the outside of a fire house,
1841.

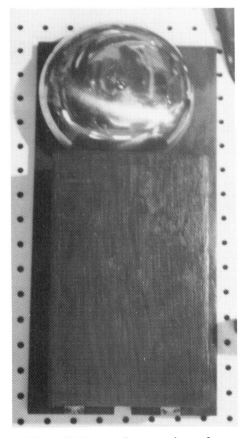

This 6" Brass Gong w/wood
case was mounted in a volunteer fireman's home.

Alarm Apparatus for Firehouses

12" Gamewell Electro-mechanical Gong w/oak case.

Visual Indicator w/oak case and 8" continuous ringing bell.

Gamewell Electro-mechanical Gong, 12" Excelsior Bronze Gong w/fancy oak case.

8" Gamewell Alarm Bell w/ chrome bell.

Alarm Apparatus for Firehouses

Gamewell 15" Electro-mechanical
Gong w/visual indicator.

Gamewell 18" Electro-mechanical
Gong w/plain oak case.

10" Electro-mechanical Gong.

Gamewell electro-mechanical
gong with carved walnut case.

Alarm Apparatus for Firehouses

Gamewell 6" Excelsior
electro-mechanical gong.

Municipal Fire & Police Telegraph Co. Fire Alarm Gong, 6"
Gong w/oak case.

Gamewell Ideal Punch Register, Excelsior Bronze w/
beveled glass top & ends, Note: has removable cup to
catch punchings.

Punch Register w/take up reel.

Alarm Apparatus for Firehouses

PRICE GUIDE FOR ALARM APPARATUS

Gamewell excelsior electro-mechanical gong:
6" - $1200.00
8" - $1800.00
10" - $2500.00
12" - $3000.00
15" - $3500.00
18" - $4000.00
Municipal Fire & Police Telegraph Co., 6" fire alarm gong, plain oak case - $1100.00
Gamewell 6" Excelsior electro-mechanical gong – $1200.00
Gamewell plain visual indicator - $2250.00
Gamewell upright call bell - $275.00
Gamewell visual indicator w/8" continous ringing bell - $2750.00
Gamewell electro-mechanical gong with carved walnut case - $3000.00
Gamewell visual indicator w/electro-mechanical gong:
8" - $3500.00
12" - $4500.00
15" - $7000.00
18" rare - $8500.00
Gamewell turtle gong:
6" - $125.00
10" - $185.00
Umbrella tapper 5" - $375.00
Boston shelf tapper 5" - $325.00
Toronto tapper 6" - $350.00
Gamewell direct acting tapper with chrome bell - $165.00
Gamewell take-up reel - $195.00
Gamewell excelsior punch register - $395.00
Arrest alarm punch register - $250.00
Horni punch register, 1930's - $375.00
Gamewell excelsior time & date stamp - $425.00
Engine house clock - $650.00-850.00
Fire alarm bell, manually operated, 12" dia. brass bell, originally
    mounted outside an engine house, 1841 - $350.00
Bell striking machine - $1200.00
Automatic whistle blowing machine - $1200.00
Semaphore - $550.00
Gamewell Diaphone - $95.00
Punch register with take-up reel - $500.00

Gamewell visual
indicator.

Gamewell 6" Excelsior
electro-mechanical
gong.

Alarm Boxes & Pedestals

Development of emergency signaling systems.

In 1845, New York was divided into numbered districts. Each district had a bell and a watchtower. If a watchman discovered a fire in his district, he would ring his bell so as to equal the district number. When the watchmen in nearby towers heard the signal, they would repeat by ringing their bells the same number of times. Eventually, the alarm was received by the proper responders. This method of signaling a fire or other emergency was slow and inefficient.

About this time, the telegraph was beginning to be used. Invented by Samuel F. B. Morse, this system allowed signals to be sent long distances over wires, by electric transmission.

Based on Morse's work, Dr. William F. Channing and Professor Moses G. Farmer, invented the fire alarm telegraph in 1847. By 1851, the first fire alarm telegraph was installed in the city of Boston.

In 1855, John N. Gamewell and James Dunlop purchased the rights and patents from Channing & Farmer. Shortly after the Civil War, the Gamewell Fire Alarm Telegraph Company was founded. By the first World War, the Gamewell Company was producing more than 95% of all fire alarm telegraph systems in the U.S..

Fire alarm telegraph systems are rather complex. Basically they consisted of four parts, fire alarm boxes, alarm apparatus, central station equipment and circuits. Fire alarm boxes were placed in various locations and provided the means for the public to transmit alarms. Alarm apparatus consisted of devices in the firehouse that alerted firefighters of a fire and the exact location. Central station equipment received signals from boxes and could transmit signals to firehouse alarms. Circuits consisted of aerial or ground wiring and formed the connecting link between the fire alarm boxes and the firehouse.

Fire alarm boxes.

Early fire alarm boxes were made of wood and were actuated by cranking a handle. The crank was attached to a code wheel which turned along with the crank. The telegraph circuit would open and close by the grouped number of teeth cut into the code wheel. Thus, the box number could be transmitted to the receiving station. These early boxes proved troublesome.

Soon, clockwork boxes that could be manually wound were designed. These boxes used a pull hook to start the operation of the clockwork. Unfortunately, if the hook was pulled more than once, the signal could become jumbled. The next box to be designed had a hook that disengaged after pulling, thereby eliminating a jumbled signal.

Still, trouble could arise if two boxes on the same circuit were actuated at the same time. In 1871, Gamewell came out with the first non-interference box. This arrangement allowed the first box actuated to send its signal while blocking out the second box.

Most street boxes were locked and required a key to actuate them. Keys were usually held by firemen, policemen and trustworthy citizens. In 1875, the keyless door was invented by R. M. Tooker. Instead of a key, a large handle could be turned to open the door. When the door was opened, a bell would ring. This discouraged false alarms and abolished the frantic searches that were sometimes required to find someone with a key.

The successive fire alarm box was invented in 1889. This box, if pulled while another box was running, was not locked out. It could run idle until the first box finished its signal. At this time, the second box would send its signal. If additional boxes were actuated, they would wait their turn and then transmit. Many other improvements were made in fire alarm boxes over the years. Examples include the Smith Key Guard, Cole Key Guard, first peerless box in 1916 and the first quick acting door in 1922.

Early boxes were made of wood and then of cast iron. The first cast iron cottage style fire alarm boxes by Gamewell were marked American Fire Alarm Telegraph and had the date of manufacture cast into the box instead of the familiar fist and lightning bolt logo. Cast iron was used until 1928 on Gamewell boxes. After this date, herculite was used in the construction of fire alarm boxes. Herculite was a die cast, silicon-aluminum alloy that was lighter and stronger than cast iron. In the 1950's, Gamewell modernized the design of the fire alarm box by creating a three piece box for easier servicing and mounting.

Certain types of fire alarm boxes had a glass window, instruction sign, key guard, crank handle, location light, or emergency phone. A few examples of fire alarm boxes had decorative designs cast into the door or outer shell. Some alarm boxes had the design of a bell, helmet, fire truck or city seal cast into the box. The Gamewell Excelsior Box had torches on a rounded door, while the Gaynor Fire Alarm Box featured a beautifully embellished arched top.

There were dozens of manufacturers of fire alarm boxes. The following is a list of the more famous companies: Gamewell, Faraday Electric, Garl Electric, Gaynor Electric, Star Electric, Horni Signal Manufacturing, Loper Fire Alarm Co., L. W. Bills Co., Municipal Fire and Police Telegraph Co., Pierce & Jones Fire Alarm Telegraph Co., Superior American Fire Alarm & Signal Co. (SAFA), Utica Fire Alarm Telegraph Co. and the Western Electric Co.

Alarm Boxes & Pedestals

Fire alarm box pedestals.

Iron pedestals were used to support fire alarm boxes in districts where underground wiring was present. Basically, a pedestal consisted of a base, post, and box holder. Many pedestals made for Gamewell had very ornate box holders and decorative finials. Needless to say, these pedestals have become quite desirable.

The JCR post featured a decorative base with a torch finial and was popular in New York City during the teens and twenties. In the 1930's, an Art Deco style post appeared. Many pedestals had a column for street light globes while other pedestals had a provision for both fire and police boxes. Later style posts were rather plain and are still fairly common.

FIRE ALARM APPARATUS.

FIRE ALARM BOXES.

FIG. 158.
No. 1 Box Closed.

We manufacture a number of Fire Alarm Signal Boxes of various construction and patterns.

No. 1 Box consists of a very fine automatic, made with the utmost care and mechanical skill, mounted in cast iron, dust tight case, all the parts of which are carefully insulated electrically from the iron, this being mounted in an inner case which contains bell magnet, signalling key two line switches for grounding either leg, of the line, or shutting the box out of service ; a lightning arrester of the best pattern, a shunt switch for cutting out the resistance of magnet when not in use, which is arranged to automatically operated bell when lever is pulled, or when signalling key is used.

FIG. 159.
No. 1 Box Open.

This case is closed by iron door with Lock and Master Key, and is mounted in the outside box, also of iron, for further protection from the weather. The outside box is secured by our patented improved, well made brass trap lock, which not only secures the key in the lock, but also covers the screws which fasten lock to door, thereby preventing it from being removed.

Alarm Boxes & Pedestals

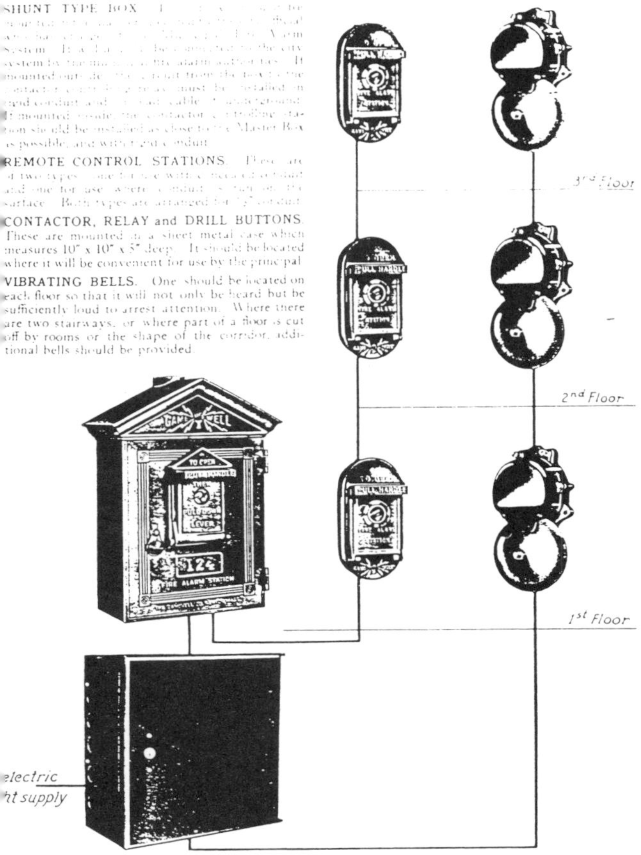

FIRE ALARM BOXES IN SERVICE

GAMEWELL DESIGNS

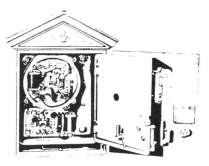

Standard Box with
First Quick Acting Door
1922

Improved Peerless Fire Alarm Box
1922

MATERIALS EMPLOYED: The materials used in fire alarm box cases are stated as follows in chronological order:

Outside Cases: Cast iron until 1928. Die cast silicon—aluminum alloy—trade name "Herculite", thereafter.

Inside Cases: Cast iron until 1922. Porcelain enamel, 1922-1928. Bakelite, 1928-1929. "Herculite" since 1929.

FIRE ALARM BOX, PEERLESS SUCCESSIVE TYPE

Photo 6780-8

FOR FIRE
BREAK GLASS
OPEN DOOR
PULL HANDLE
DOWN ONCE
LET GO
315

Standard with
Cole Keyguard
1946

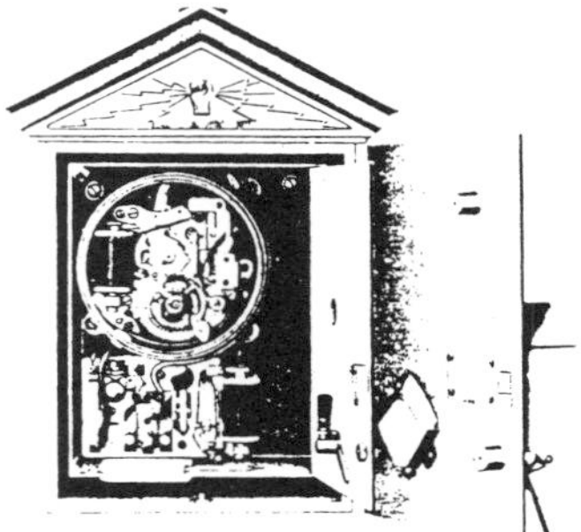

First Peerless Fire Alarm Box
1916

Photo 6780

Door-Opening Type

KEYLESS DOORS
With Local Alarm Bell, Manually Operative

Self-Starting Type

NOTE: Parts for keyless doors are no longer available but doors may be replaced by the modern quick-action type—with or without Arrestolarms—the local alarm devices now employed to discourage false alarms.

SHUNT TYPE BOX. [...text partially illegible...] Fire Alarm System. It is that a box connected to the city system by the means of its alarm authorities. It is mounted out of doors a foot from the box's the contact assembly must be installed in rigid conduit and in that cable is not enclosed. If mounted inside the contactor and building station should be installed as close to the Master Box as possible and with rigid conduit.

REMOTE CONTROL STATIONS. These are of two types—one for use with a flush conduit and one for use where conduit is run on the surface. Both types are arranged for rigid conduit.

CONTACTOR, RELAY and DRILL BUTTONS. These are mounted in a sheet metal case which measures 10" x 10" x 5" deep. It should be located where it will be convenient for use by the principal.

VIBRATING BELLS. One should be located on each floor so that it will not only be heard but be sufficiently loud to arrest attention. Where there are two stairways, or where part of a floor is cut off by rooms or the shape of the corridor, additional bells should be provided.

FIRE ALARM BOX, PEERLESS SUCCESSIVE TYPES

Photo 6780-12

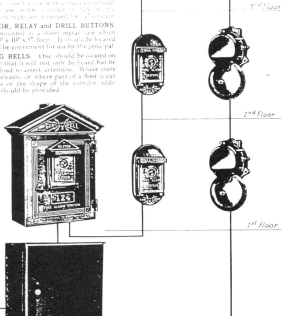

3rd Floor

2nd Floor

1st Floor

electric
light supply

Peerless,
1928 Design

Peerless Master Box
1928 Design

FIRE ALARM BOX, PEERLESS SUCCESSIVE TYPE

Photo 6780-11

Standard with
Quick Action Door
1924

Standard with
Quick Action Door and White Stripe
1931

Original Catalog Pages

Alarm Boxes & Pedestals

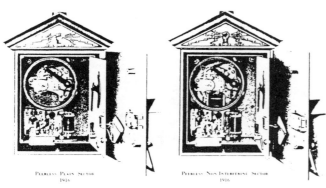

PEERLESS PLAIN SECTOR
1916

PEERLESS NON-INTERFERING SECTOR
1916

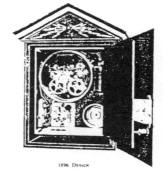
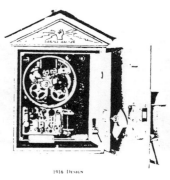

1896 Design

1916 Design

FIRE ALARM BOXES, IDEAL TYPES

Photo 6780-7

FOR FIRE
BREAK GLASS
OPEN DOOR
PULL HARD
ONCE
LET GO

315

STANDARD WITH
COLE KEYGUARD
1901

SILENT TAPE MASTER BOX
1916

FIRE ALARM BOX, GARDINER NON-INTERFERING TYPE

Photo 6780-3

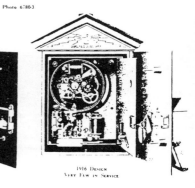

1887 Design

1916 Design
VERY FEW IN SERVICE

FIRE ALARM BOX, EXCELSIOR NON-INTERFERING TYPES

Photo 6780-6

NI EXCELSIOR FIRE ALARM BOX
1901

PNI EXCELSIOR FIRE ALARM BOX
1904

FIRE ALARM BOX, WEIGHT SECTOR, NON-INTERFERING TYPE

Photo 6780-2

1883 Design

FIRE ALARM BOX, EXCELSIOR INTERFERING TYPE

Photo 6780-5

FIRE ALARM
TELEGRAPH
STATION

43

1900 DESIGN WITH COLE KEYGUARDED ADDED

NO. 4 SECTOR FIRE ALARM BOX

Photo 6780-1

FIRE ALARM
TELEGRAPH
STATION

26

FIRE
ALARM
FIRE ALARM

26

SOLID DOOR
1880

IMPROVED PORCELAIN INSULATION
1916

HALF GLASS DOOR
1880

Original Catalog Pages

Alarm Boxes & Pedestals

Type "B" Pedestals

No. 623

No. 624

Fire Alarm Box and Police Box Pedestal

No. 623 Peerless, Ideal, or Gardiner box with
Standard police box, with column for
two lights. Space for terminals provided in base.

No. 624 Peerless, Ideal, or Gardiner box with
Standard police box, with column for
three lights. Space for terminals provided in base.

Can be adapted for Excelsior or Sector Fire Alarm Boxes or Exemplar Police Box

Type "B" Pedestals

Front View   Side View

No. 617   **No. 617**   **No. 636**

Alarm Box and Terminal Box Pedestal   **Terminal Post**

No. 617 Peerless, Ideal, or Gardiner box with terminal box.   **No. 636** Terminal post for
test purposes.

No. 618 Standard police box with terminal box.   **No. 637** Same style post as
No. 636, except that
base is same as
shown on No. 625,
page 3, Type "A".

Can be adapted for Excelsior or Sector Fire Alarm Boxes or Exemplar Police Box

Type "C" Pedestals

Plain Type Top Post

(Illustration at left)

No. 702 Peerless, Ideal, or Gardiner fire alarm box, with cable
box below.

No. 701 Same as No. 702, except ladder holder and mushroom
top in place of globe.

No. 722 Same as No. 702, with long cable box with door on back.

No. 721 Same as No. 702, except ladder rest and mushroom top
in place of globe, and with long cable box with door on
back.

Split Type Top Post

(Illustration at right)

No. 705 Peerless, Ideal, or Gardiner fire alarm box, with cable
box beneath.

No. 704 Same as No. 705, except ladder rest and mushroom top
in place of globe.

No. 725 Same as No. 705, with long cable box with door on back.

No. 724 Same as No. 705, except ladder rest and mushroom top
in place of globe, and with long cable box with door on
back.

No. 702   **No. 705**

Type "B" Pedestals

Front View   Side View

No. 617   **No. 617**   **No. 636**

Alarm Box and Terminal Box Pedestal   **Terminal Post**

No. 617 Peerless, Ideal, or Gardiner box with terminal box.   **No. 636** Terminal post for
test purposes.

No. 618 Standard police box with terminal box.   **No. 637** Same style post as
No. 636, except that
base is same as
shown on No. 625,
page 3, Type "A".

Can be adapted for Excelsior or Sector Fire Alarm Boxes or Exemplar Police Box

Original Catalog Pages

Alarm Boxes & Pedestals

Type "C" Pedestals

No. 700

No. 703

No. 708

Plain Top Post

No. 700 Peerless, Ideal, or Gardiner fire alarm box, with cable box below.

No. 706 Same as No. 700, except that it has shelf for fastening in place of leaded joint.

No. 720 Same as No. 700, with long cable box with door on back.

Split Type Top Post

No. 703 Peerless, Ideal, or Gardiner fire alarm box, with cable box below.

No. 723 Same as No. 703, with long cable box on back.

Plain Top Post Shelf Support

No. 708 Peerless, Ideal, or Gardiner fire alarm box, with cable box below.

No. 707 Same as No. 708, except ladder rest and mushroom top in place of globe.

Type "B" Pedestals

View Showing Police Box

Side View

View showing Fire Alarm Box

No. 619   No. 619   No. 619

Fire Alarm Box and Police Box Pedestal

No. 619 Peerless, Ideal, or Gardiner box with Standard police box

Can be adapted for Excelsior or Sector Fire Alarm Boxes or Exemplar Police Box

Various Parts of Pedestals

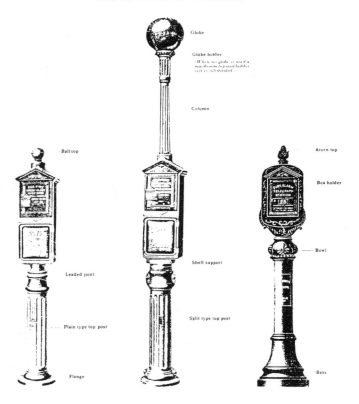

Globe

Globe holder

When no globe is used a mushroom top and ladder rest is substituted.

Column

Ball top

Acorn top

Box holder

Leaded joint

Shelf support

Bowl

Plain type top post

Split type top post

Base

Flange

Ground extension is the section from the sidewalk down

UMBRIA CLOCK

Umbria Clock with Electrical Contacts for Testing Fire Alarm System

Alarm Boxes & Pedestals

Fire Alarm Box Post, Art
Deco, 1930's.

Ornate Gamewell pedestal
with alarm box.

JCR Post w/torch finial,
1912.

Gamewell Herculite
Fire Alarm Box, 1940's.

Gamewell Fire Alarm Box
w/quick acting door.

Alarm Boxes & Pedestals

Gamewell Arch Type Fire Alarm Box w/
Cole keyguard, 1905.

Interior view of Gamewell Herculite Fire Alarm Box,
1940's.

Left - Gamewell Cast Iron Fire Alarm Box
w/quick acting door.
Right - Gamewell Remote Pull Station.

Gamewell Fire Alarm Station
from a Hospital.

Alarm Boxes & Pedestals

Autocall Co. Fire Alarm Box.

Gamewell Oval Style Fire Alarm Box.

Garl Fire Alarm Box w/Plain
Pedestal.

Two Styles of Alarm Box
Pedestals.

Alarm Boxes & Pedestals

PRICE GUIDE FOR ALARM BOXES & PEDESTALS

American fire alarm box (early Gamewell), 1870 - $1800.00
Bills fire alarm box - $200.00
Chicago alarm box, cast iron - $300.00
Gamewell cast iron fire alarm box, 1920's - $250.00
Gamewell herculite box, 1940's - $150.00
Gamewell excelsior box, arch top, 1900 - $300.00
Gamewell sector box w/half glass door, 1880 - $300.00
Gamewell three-fold box, 1950's - $125.00
Gamewell remote pull station, cottage syle - $175.00
Gaynor Electric Co. fire alarm box - cast iron with arched top, rare – $1500.00+
Ornate Gamewell pedestal with alarm box – $750.00
Fire Alarm box key with original stamped metal tag by Gamewell – $350.00
Horni fire alarm box, 1930's - $175.00
SAFA fire alarm box – $150.00
SAFA fire alarm box and pedestal – $600.00
Sector box FDNY – $200.00
Star electric fire alarm box - $1250.00
Fire alarm sign, porcelain on steel, red & white w/arrow and words fire alarm 4" x 12" - $65.00
Fire toy alarm box and lamp post – $35.00
Fire alarm box key – $50.00

Pedestal pricing.
Plain alarm box pedestal - $150.00-250.00
Ornate pedestal with decorative finial - $450.00+
Ornate pedestal w/column & street light globes - $1200.00+

Grouping of fire alarm box related collectibles:

Fire alarm box key w/orig. stamped metal tag by Gamewell.

Sector box FDNY.

Fire toy alarm box & lamp post.

Fire alarm box key.

SAFA fire alarm box and pedestal.

Gaynor Electric Co. fire alarm box - cast iron with arched top, rare.
Note: Door was modified at one time; probably with a quick acting device and key guard. Box has been re-painted red.

Art, Lithographs, Prints & Posters

Art.

Firemen of old hired artists to paint beautiful scenes and designs on early apparatus. Found mainly in museums, engine panels with works of art are rare today. Over the years, countless artists have created paintings, drawings, statues, sculptures and other forms of art devoted to a fire-related theme. The sheer volume of artwork available to collect makes it easy to obtain many modern items for a collection. The rule of thumb for collectors is to collect works of art that appeal to them personally.

Lithographs, prints and posters.

In the early 1800's, pictures in books and newspapers were difficult to reproduce. Conventional methods such as woodcuts or copperplate engravings were painstakingly slow. In America, a new process called lithography was being learned. Invented in 1795 by a Bavarian named Alois Senefelder, lithography was a process of printing from a soft stone plate.

The stone was a special type of slate which was cut rectangular and ground smooth. An artist or lithographer would use water-repelling crayons to sketch a design or lettering directly on the stone.

Next, the stone was immersed in an acid bath. Any area on the stone not protected by the crayons would dissolve, thus leaving the crayon design in relief.

The stone was then wet thoroughly with water and placed in a press. A special grease-like ink would be applied by a roller. The ink would be absorbed by the crayon and repelled by the wet, recessed areas of the stone. Paper was then applied to the inked plate with pressure and a print was created. The print could then be hand colored.

The firm of Currier and Ives was famous for the thousands of prints it produced using lithography from 1866 to 1907. Prints were made in a variety of sizes from about 3" x 5" to the large folio size which measured approximately 18" x 27". Some of the company's work was directed toward creating prints related to firefighting and certificates used by fire companies.

Currier and Ives employed skilled artists who helped create "The Life of a Fireman" series, "American Fireman" series and the "Darktown" series. Nathaniel Currier, dressed in a fireman's uniform posed for the print "The American Fireman. Always Ready". Many others produced fire related prints such as Buchanan & Lyall's "Firemen, Past and Present" series.

Prints that originally sold for six cents apiece are worth hundreds of dollars today. Many prints have been reproduced or restruck. One method to distinguish a modern reproduction from an old lithograph is to examine the print under magnification. Modern printing shows as small, perfectly formed dots, whereas 19th century lithography does not. Tears, stains, fading and trimmed edges all reduce the value of a print. It is best to consult a reputable dealer when purchasing an original, antique print.

Posters related to firefighting is another area of collecting. Many posters were a form of advertising and poster art often mirrored the era in which it was created. The Brothers Byrne Circus poster featuring comic firemen, a steam fire engine and a human staircase was produced in 1898 and is highly collectible. Movie posters such as "Night Alarm", "Towering Inferno" and "Backdraft" are Hollywood's contributions to firefighting collectibles. Other posters that have raised an eyebrow or two, feature scantily clad young women posed with firefighting gear.

Art, Lithographs, Prints & Posters

"The Firefighter" Fireman with hose & nozzle on sheet copper.

Fireman Statue, 16 1/2" Tall.

Chalk Statue of a Fireman Standing Next to a Hydrant, Painted gold & black, 27" Tall.

Composition Statue of Fireman Saving Child, 26 1/2" Tall.

Spelter composition statue of a fireman holding a trumpet.

Spelter Composition Statue of a Fireman Rescuing a Child, Descending a Ladder, 31" Tall.

Art, Lithographs, Prints & Posters

THE LIFE OF A FIREMAN
THE METROPOLITAN SYSTEM

Top & Bottom - Prints from Currier & Ives "The Life of a Fireman" series.

THE LIFE OF A FIREMAN

THE RUINS.—"TAKE UP." "MAN YOUR ROPE."

Art, Lithographs, Prints & Posters

THE AMERICAN FIREMAN
RUSHING TO THE CONFLICT.

"The American Fireman - Rushing to the Conflict", print by Currier & Ives.

THE AMERICAN FIREMAN.
PROMPT TO THE RESCUE.

"The American Fireman - Prompt to the Rescue", print by Currier & Ives.

Art, Lithographs, Prints & Posters

"The American Fireman - Always Ready",
print by Currier & Ives.

"The American Fireman - Facing the Enemy",
print by Currier & Ives.

Art, Lithographs, Prints & Posters

"The Race - Jump Her Boys, Jump Her",
print by Currier & Ives.

"The Little Fireman", print by Currier & Ives.

"The Night Alarm, Start Her Lively Boys",
print by Currier & Ives.

"Hot Stuff" poster.

Art, Lithographs, Prints & Posters

PRICE GUIDE FOR ART, LITHOGRAPHS, PRINTS & POSTERS

Art.
Composition statue of fireman saving child, 26 1/2" tall - $3000.00
Fireman statue, 16 1/2" tall - $2500.00
The Firefighter, fireman with hose & nozzle on sheet copper - $165.00
Spelter composition statue of fireman saving child descending a ladder, 31" tall - $3000.00
Spelter composition statue of a fireman holding a trumpet – $3500.00+
Chalk statue of fireman standing next to hydrant, 27" tall - $3500.00

Currier & Ives Prints.
"The Life of a Fireman" series (Large folio)
The Fire. "Now then with a will - Shake her up boys!" - $4500.00
The Metropolitan System - $6500.00+
The New Era. Steam and Muscle - $4500.00
The Night Alarm. "Start her lively boys" - $4750.00
The Race. "Jump her boys, jump her!" - $4500.00
The Ruins. "Take up - Man your rope" - $4500.00
"The American Fireman" series (Medium folio)
Always Ready - $3500.00
Facing the Enemy - $3500.00
Prompt to the Rescue - $3500.00
Rushing to the Conflict - $3500.00
"Fire" series
Burning of the New York Crystal Palace, on Tuesday, Oct. 5th, 1858 - $1800.00
The Great Fire at Boston, November 9th & 10th, 1872 - $500.00
The Great Fire at St. John, N.B., June 20th, 1877 - $450.00
The Great Conflagration, Pittsburgh, PA (Small folio) - $1000.00
"The Darktown Fire Brigade" series (Small folio)
Saved! - $350.00
To the Rescue - $350.00
A Prize Squirt - $400.00
The Last Shake - $325.00
Hook & Ladder Gymnastics - $350.00
Slightly Demoralized - $325.00
Investigating a Smoke - $350.00
Taking a Rest - $300.00
Under Full Steam - $350.00
The Foreman on Parade - $325.00
The Chief on Duty - $325.00
All on their Mettle - $325.00
"The Darktown Hook & Ladder Corps" series
In Action (Small folio) - 350.00, (Large folio) - $800.00
Going to the Front (Small folio) - $325.00, (Large folio) - $750.00
Currier & Ives Fireman's certificates - $400.00-500.00
"The Little Fireman" print by Currier & Ives - $900.00

Buchanan & Lyall Prints.
"Firemen, Past & Present" series
Cut Her Loose Boys - $1000.00-1200.00
Let Her Go - $1000.00-1200.00
Start for Home - $1000.00-1200.00
The Old and the New - $1000.00-1200.00
Up to Date - $1000.00-1200.00
Wrap Her Up - $1000.00-1200.00

Poster Pricing.
Brothers Byrne Circus Poster - $450.00
Towering Inferno (30" x 40") - $95.00 (14" x 22") - $65.00
Backdraft - $40.00
Hot Stuff Poster - $20.00

Avon Items

Sought after by Avon collectors as well as fire buffs is a group of Avon items in a firemanic theme. Who would imagine the rarest of these items is fire engine soap. Made in 1957, this red soap was molded in the shape of a fire engine, and came in a red box. Originally selling for 59 cents, it is now worth $75.00, if found mint in it's original box. Soap that is used, damaged, or missing the box is worthless and should not be purchased.

Easier to locate is a group of five cologne/after shave bottles molded in clear glass and painted. The earliest is the First Volunteer cologne bottle. Made in 1971-1972, this bottle's shape is that of a steam fire engine. This six ounce bottle is painted gold, with a gold plastic front covering the cap.

The "Fire Alarm Box" appeared in 1975 and was made thru 1976. It is a red painted glass bottle in the shape of an alarm box with a black plastic cap. It holds four ounces of product.

Produced at the same time as the "Fire Alarm Box" was the "No Parking Fire Plug". This bottle is in the shape of a fire hydrant. It holds six ounces of product and has a red plastic cap.

The next Avon bottle to appear was "The Fire Fighter" in 1975. This red painted bottle resembled a 1910 American LaFrance Pumper. It has a red plastic rear hosebed that covers the cap. This six ounce bottle contained "Wild Country After Shave". Interestingly there is a warning label on the bottom of this bottle which states, "Caution: flammable until dry".

The "Red Sentinel" was the latest bottle made by Avon in a fire related theme. This bottle is a four piece design in the shape of a fire ladder truck. Part of the bottle holds after shave and another part holds talc. This bottle is also clear glass painted red and was produced in 1978-79.

It is best to collect full bottles with the original box. Be wary of bottles with missing front or rear plastic cap covers. Avon fire bottles are inexpensive items to include in your collection.

Probably the most handsome item was the firefighter's stein. This item, made in 1989 was the last fire related item Avon produced. Made of ceramic, this nine inch stein had a steamer design and a gold bell lid.

Avon Items

Avon First Volunteer Cologne
Bottle, six ounce, painted gold,
1971-72.

Avon Fire Alarm
Box, four ounce,
painted red,
1975-76.

Avon No Parking
Fire Plug, six
ounce, painted
red, 1975-76.

Avon Firefighter's Stein, ceramic
with gold bell lid, 1989.

Avon 1910 Fire Fighter, six ounce,
painted red, 1975.

PRICE GUIDE FOR AVON ITEMS

(Mint condition in the box)

Fire Engine Soap - $85.00
First Volunteer - $20.00
Fire Alarm Box - $12.00
No Parking Fire Plug - $12.00

The Fire Fighter - $17.50
Red Sentinel - $20.00
Fire Fighter's Stein - $40.00
The Fire Fighter - $18.00

Axes

The fire axe has proved to be, over the years, one of a fireman's most useful and favorite tools. It's unique head has two ends. The pick end comes to a point and is used for prying. The other end has a blade and is used for chopping. Often times a fireman is ordered to "open a roof". This refers to chopping a hole in the roof above the fire to let smoke and hot gases escape from inside the structure. Search and rescue operations along with fire extinguishment are greatly improved by this action.

Fire axes were made in many different sizes, ranging from small hatchet sizes to large "viking" style axes. Viking style axes, or battle axes as they are sometimes referred to, have a fan like blade and frequently feature a curved handle. Particularly desirable are 19th Century parade axes. These axes were constructed mainly of wood and were highly decorated. Parade axes were less expensive to issue to the entire fire company and were light weight. Many a proud fireman carried these axes in parades, hence the term parade axe.

Axe heads were typically made of iron or steel. They could be painted, bronzed, nickel or chromium plated. Handles were made of wood and frequently had painted ends.

When looking for an axe, check for any cracks or damage to the axe head. Note if the handle has been changed or refinished. Many current fire axes are being made with fiberglass handles and are far stronger than their old wooden handle counterparts.

A FUN WAY OF SHOWING YOUR COLLECTION

An engine house in your own backyard! Richard Bosanko of the
Kenosha, Wisconsin Fire Department gave up his
garage to house fire fighting collectibles.

FIRE HATCHET.

Hatchets. . . . .   Fire Axes. . . . .

FIRE AXE, WITH PICK HEAD.

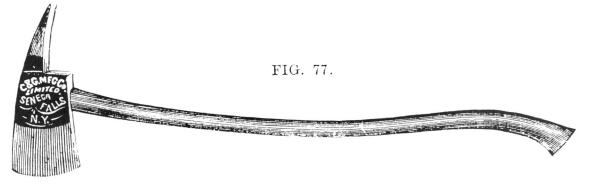

FIG. 77.

Large size—handle painted—head of axe bronzed.

Fire Axe, with Pick Head.

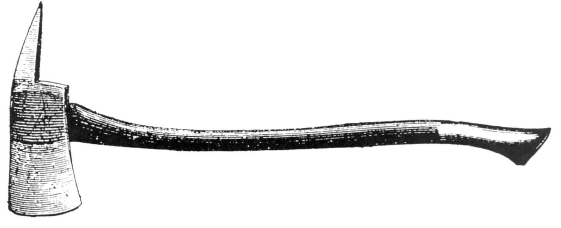

Large size—handle painted—head of axe bronzed,

Axes

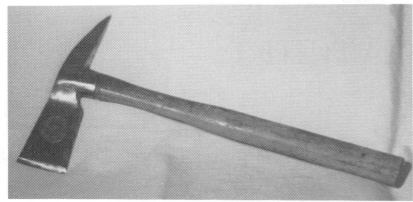

Fire Axe, small version.

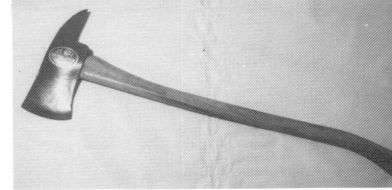

Standard Fire Axe "Indian Chief".

Parade Axe, Viking style.

Viking Style Fire Axe, 1850.

Price Guide for Axes

Fire Axe, standard - $40-65
Fire Axe, small style - $25-50
Viking style axe - $350-400
Parade Axe, plain wood - $150-250
Parade Axe, 1800's, decorated - $900-1750

Badges

Badges have been used since the 14th century when knights wore them in battle as marks of identification. It wasn't until the 1840's that badges were worn by firemen as a means of identification at a fire. These early badges were made of german silver or brass and were typically shield, round or oval shaped. The fire company's name was hand engraved on the badge. An old badge engraved H. & L. stands for hook and ladder. The badge was attached to the uniform by a pin with a wire loop. Mid 19th Century badges, with hand engraving, are very valuable and scarce.

By the 1870's badges were being produced by stock dies. Stock die badges had areas on the badge that lettering could be added. Often times these badges had blank centers whereby different designs could be affixed at the department's request. Stock die badges were a kind of generic badge, and were relatively inexpensive to produce.

Custom die badges were also available. These badges were created especially for a particular fire department. Many badges featured raised lettering and one of a kind designs. The workmanship was usually of a higher caliber than stock die badges. Custom die badges are more desirable because they were produced in limited numbers and were more expensive to produce.

Many badges featured apparatus, helmets, hose and other equipment. Later badges may have the maltese cross, the eagle or the phoenix as part of the design. Many men have worn these badges without knowing the origins of these designs.

The maltese cross symbolizes the open wings of a bird protecting its young. Originally used by Christian Knights who protected the weak, it now represents the protecting power of the men and women of the fire service. The eagle represents authority and good judgement which is essential in any emergency situation. The phoenix originally was a representation by early Christians as the resurrection of Christ. It is also used to symbolize the resurrection of a city destroyed by fire.

Various types of metals and finishes were used on badges. Examples include gold, silver or rhodium plating. In many instances, a presentation badge was given to a honored member. These badges could be made of solid silver or gold.

Another collectible badge is the fire lines badge. This type of badge was issued to reporters and city officials and permitted access to a fire scene.

Badge collecting is a field of its own with thousands of variations in design to collect.

Badges

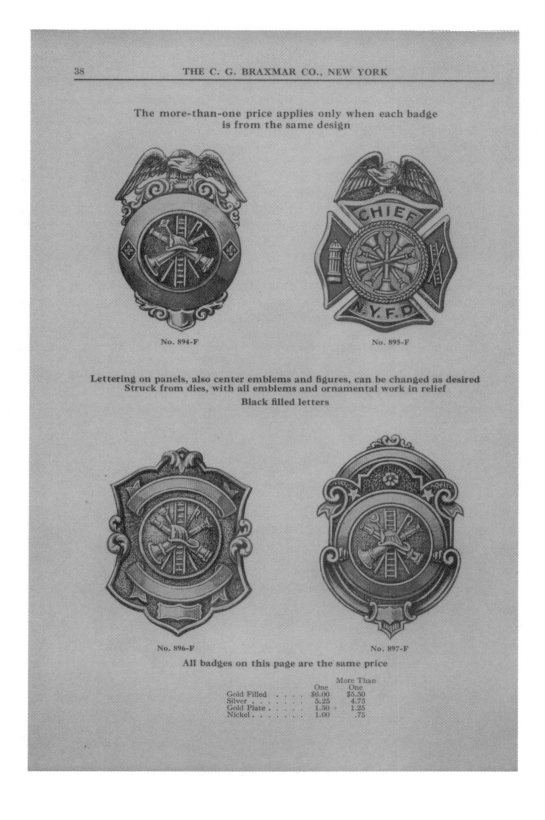

The more-than-one price applies only when each badge
is from the same design

No. 894-F   No. 895-F

Lettering on panels, also center emblems and figures, can be changed as desired
Struck from dies, with all emblems and ornamental work in relief

Black filled letters

No. 896-F   No. 897-F

All badges on this page are the same price

	One	More Than One
Gold Filled	$6.00	$5.50
Silver	5.25	4.75
Gold Plate	1.50	1.25
Nickel	1.00	.75

1921 Original Catalog Page

Badges

The more-than-one price applies only when each badge
is from the same design

No. 927-F   No. 928-F

Lettering, also center emblems or numbers as desired
Black filled letters

No. 929-F   No. 930-F

All badges on this page are the same price

		More Than
	One	One
Gold Filled	$7.00	$6.50
Silver	6.00	5.50
Gold Plate	2.00	1.75
Nickel	1.25	1.00

1921 Original Catalog Page

Badges

B623
Available either with stenciled
solid panel at bottom
or applied cut-out figures on open back

B1060
Badges B1060, B720 and B687 supplied with
Roman lettering unless otherwise specified.
Be sure to order block lettering if desired

B720

B624
Available only with applied figures
on solid pebbled back.
Limit of four figures.

B687

B887
Star center in die. Any lettering desired around rim.
15/16" center may be applied over center. Available only
with bottom panel stenciled solid panel. Open back not
available this style.

B630

B750

B625

Badges

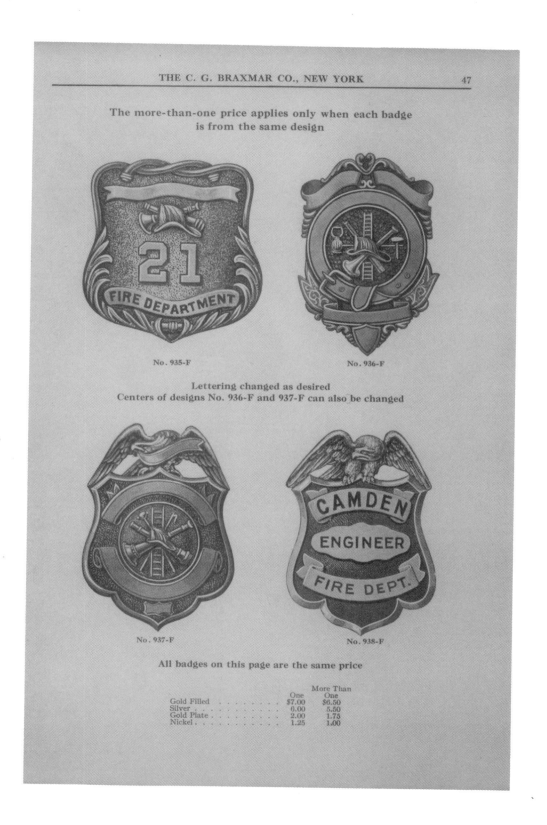

The more-than-one price applies only when each badge
is from the same design

No. 935-F

No. 936-F

Lettering changed as desired
Centers of designs No. 936-F and 937-F can also be changed

No. 937-F

No. 938-F

All badges on this page are the same price

	One	More Than One
Gold Filled	$7.00	$6.50
Silver	6.00	5.50
Gold Plate	2.00	1.75
Nickel	1.25	1.00

1921 Original Catalog Page

Badges

S. F. HAYWARD & CO.

BADGES.

Plate 268.
Style No. 131.
Size, 2¼x1½ inches.
Nickel..............
Gilt.................

Plate 269.
Style No. 145.
Size, 2½x1⅞ inches.
Nickel..............
Gilt.................

Plate 270.
Style No. 130.
Size, 1⅜x1⅜ inches.
Nickel..............
Gilt.................

Plate 271.
Style, No. 129.
Size, 1⅝x1½ inches.
Nickel..............
Gilt.................

Plate 272.
Style No. 197.
Size, 2¼x1¾ inches.
Nickel..............

Plate 273.
Style No. 127.
Size, 1¾x1¾ inches.
Nickel..............
Gilt.................

Badges.

STAR PATTER

This badge is made
three styles, plain
for privates ; with rib
on top for Foremen
Assistants ; and w
eagle on top for Comm
ioners. Chiefs and Sup
intendents.

Made of German Sil
and Plated or Oro
Metal and Gilt, lett
engraved by hand, a
blacked in, numb
soldered on ; or
place of the numb
emblems, same as
shield pattern Bac
shown below.

EAC

Plain Star -
With ribbon on top,
With eagle on top,

SHIELD PATTERN.

This style Badge is also furnished,
plain shield, and with ribbon or eagle
on top.

EACH.

Plain Shield, lettered, - -
With ribbon, - - -
With eagle, - - -

This style is very appropriate for Chief
Engineers, Foremen of Companies or
Fire Marshals.

Badges

Badges.

No. 1. with Emblems.

No 1. with Steamer.

No 1.—Furnished with emblems, or steamer as shown in cuts ; or hand engine, hose carriage, or hook and ladder truck, as desired.

No. 15.

No 71, with Hook and Ladder Truck, or Hose Carriage.

Nos 1, 15 or 71, furnished of Silver-Plated or Oroide Metal, as shown in the cuts, without lettering, at 60 cents each, or $40 a hundred. Engraved and blacked in letters 2 cents per letter additional.

To Companies or Departments wishing a die made for a badge of special design, so that the lettering can be RAISED instead of engraved by hand, we will send samples of Badges of new and handsome designs, for selection. Dies will cost from $10 to $20 (according to amount of work on them), and the Badges made from the dies, 40 cents each, including the RAISED letters.

BADGES.

FIG. 107.

FIG. 108.

Nos. 78 and 79—Price, each ....

Estimates given on Badges of every description. Made of Gold, Silver or Oreida Metal.

FIG. 109.

FIG. 110.

Nos. 80 and 81—Price, each........   ....

BADGES.

E

Nickel . . . .
Gilt . . . .

F

Nickel . . . .
Gilt . . . .

G

Nickel . . . .
Gilt . . . .
Silver . . . .
Gold . . . .

H

Nickel . . . .
Gilt . . . .
Silver . . . .
Gold . . . .

BADGES.

A

Nickel . . . .
Gilt . . . .

B

Nickel . . . .
Gilt . . . .

C

Nickel . . . .
Gilt . . . .
Silver . . . .
Gold . . . .

D

Nickel . . . .
Gilt . . . .
Silver . . . .
Gold . . . .

Badges

FIREMEN'S BADGES FOR SERVICE USE AND PRIZES.

No. 283.

No. 284.

No. 285.   No. 286.   No. 287.

These styles of Badges are adopted by a great many cities, and are made up very handsome for **Engines, Hose or Truck Companies.** They are made of German silver or gilt metal. These cuts represent Badges the exact size.

No. 823.—This is the most approved badge now in use, and is the same shape as the New York Fire Department.

Badges in either German silver or gold, gilt styles, Nos. 284, 286, 287 and 823, with same name and number of company engraved on top and bottom.

Style No. 285, all gold or all silver gilt, with name on top and number or company on bottom or design of Engine, Hose Carriage, Hook and Ladder Truck or number in piece.

Or we can furnish the No. 285 badge, with a silver border and gold centre at the same price. we cannot sell less than 50 at the 100 price as given. We will mail sample badges on receipt of price for approval.

Badges

Gilt Oval Badge, custom die,
with German silver numbers,
Philadelphia, 1860's.

Badge w/horse drawn fire wagon,
custom die, by Braxmar.

*Courtesy of
Steven Scher*

Fire Lines Badge, 1890's.

Cross Style Badge, Brooklyn
Fire Dept.

Badges

PRICE GUIDE FOR BADGES

(#2 condition with pin)

Hand engraved, silver plated, shield-Good Intent Hose 1 B.F.D. - $295.00

Hand engraved, german silver, oval-Fireman C.F.D. (Cincinnati) - $225.00

Hand engraved, nickel plated, shield w/steamer-Welch B.F.D. - $295.00

Hand cut and chased sterling silver shield, w/engraved hook & ladder and
    #1, filled with black enamel, Woodbridge Honorary - $250.00

Custom die, nickel plated, maltese cross-S.F.F.D. circa 1880's - $225.00

Custom die, gilt oval w/german silver numbers & hose border
    Philadelphia Fire Department 1962 (Philadelphia, 1860's) - $295.00

Custom die, oval w/horse drawn wagon-Fire Patrol 336 made by Braxmar - $325.00

Custom die, german silver shield w/helmet, nozzle & trumpet at top &
    Tenton Fire Department 371 in raised letters, 1890 - $175.00

Helmet front shaped badge, german silver w/gold number Weber Hose 3 B.D.D.B. - $275.00

Oval, nickel plated badge, engraved Housewatchman #301, 1950's - $75.00

Solid gold presentation badge - $550-800

Gold plated chief's badge (modern) - $75-100

Stock die, round w/hose border, has gold fire helmet, Hoboken F.D.
    in raised letters, assistant engraved along bottom, 1860's - $225.00

Modern stock die badges - $45.00-125.00

Fire lines badge, nickel plated, N.Y.F.D. #317 - $295.00

Cross, nickel plated, B.F.D. Brooklyn Fire Dept. 951 - $225.00

Banners

During the late 1800s, Fire Companies and Exempt Associations popularized the use of banners. A banner could be used to head a parade, as a prop at a convention, or could be displayed in the firehouse. The banner was usually made of silk that was lettered and decorated with oil paint. To further embellish the banner, fringe, cords, and tassels were added. In order to support the banner, a hardwood pole was provided, which sometimes had brass ornamentation. Two typical sizes that were available were 36" x 54" and 72" x 24". Finding a nice example of a Fire Company banner can be difficult as many banners deteriorated over the years and were discarded.

Painted silk Fire Company banner with fringe and tassels – $500.00 - 2500.00

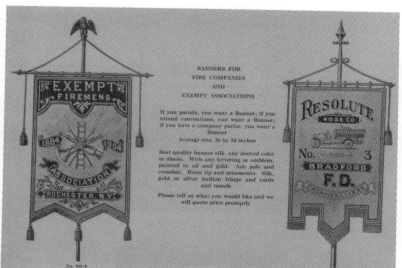

Ball, Fireman's

The annual Fireman's Ball was the largest social event of the season for many a city and town during the 800's and early 1900's. Firemen and leading citizens alike, would dress in their finest attire and dance to popular ballads in a lavishly decorated ballroom.

A great amount of paper ephemera was produced related to the Fireman's Ball. Colorful dance programs, ards, tickets, and announcements can be found with fire related illustrations. Paper items with fine color chography or engravings are the most desirable to collect. Custom paper items that were fully printed with formation are preferred over salesmen's samples or blank, generic ephemera.

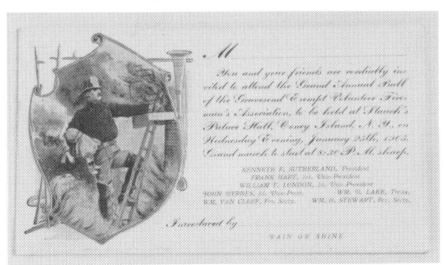

Invitational Card to a Fireman's Ball, 1905. This card was never actually sent out, making it less desirable than a complete card.

Price Guide for Fireman's Ball

Program, full color cover, featuring a horse drawn steamer, dated 1911 - $65.00
Ticket, with engraving of a horse cart, dated 1876 - $40.00
Plain Ticket, no illustration, early 1900's - $7.50-15.00
Dance Card, with horse drawn steamer, dated 1890 - $35.00
Plain Dance Card, dated 1886 - $17.50
Invitational Card w/color illustration of fireman rescuing a child, dated 1905 - $27.50

Bells, Fire Engine

Before the invention of sirens, fire wagons needed a warning device to clear the way to the fire. In about 1800, members of Philadelphia Hose #1 mounted a bell on their apparatus. The loud clanging of the bell proved effective, and its use spread to other fire companies.

Fire engine bells were usually cast in brass or bronze. They could be brightly polished or plated in nickel or chromium. They came in a variety of sizes ranging from a few inches to over 12 inches in diameter. Bells could be mounted in a fixed position or could swing freely in a bracket. When a bell was mounted in a fixed position a rope was attached to the clapper. The rope could then be pulled to cause the clapper to strike the inside of the bell. The top of the bell may have a finial in the shape of an eagle, fireman or more commonly an acorn.

Generally the most valuable bells are larger ones with nicely detailed finials. Many bells are stamped with a fire department's initials.

When examining a bell for purchase, ring it. The bell should have a sharp, clear tone. If not, check for cracks in the bell or look for a missing clapper. Examine the bracket and check for stress cracks. Fire engine bells can be rather expensive, as they are sought after by fire engine restorers as well as fire memorabilia collectors.

Bells, Fire Engine

HOSE CARRIAGE BELLS.

FIG. 51.

HALF SIZE CUT, 4½ INCH MOUTH, BELL.
PURE COPPER AND TIN BELLS. POLISHED, WITH FANCY TURNED BRASS TONGUES.

Diameter of Mouth 4½ inches each, - - - - - - - - - - - - - -
"   "   " 5¾   "   "   - - - - - - - - - - - - - -
"   "   " 7   "   "   - - - - - - - - - - - - - -

PRICES NICKLE PLATED.

Diameter of Mouth 4½ inches each, - - - - - - - - - - - - - -
"   "   " 5¾   "   "   - - - - - - - - - - - - - -
"   "   " 7   "   "   - - - - - - - - - - - - - -
Springs for above Bells, each   " - - - - - - - - - - - - - -

FIRE ALARM BELLS.

FIG 52.

All our Fire Alarm Bells are made of pure Copper and Tin. Every Bell warranted for 3 years. Prices of large Bells and Mountings on application.

Bells, Fire Engine

12" Brass Bell w/exquisite "Goddess of Liberty" finial.

8" Brass Bell w/acorn finial, probably from a hose cart.

Bronze Fire Dept. bell, 10" diameter.

12" Fire Bell, chromium plated w/eagle finial.

Bells, Fire Engine

10" – Fire Insurance Patrol Bell,
chromium plated w/bracket.

10" Fire Bell, nickel plated w/acorn finial.

Price Guide for Bells, Fire Engine

4" Brass Bell with eagle finial - $250.00
5" Hose Cart Bell - $325.00-350.00
8" Hose Cart Bell - $375.00-425.00
10" Bronze Fire Department Bell – $450.00
10" Fire Insurance Patrol Bell – $675.00
10" Bell, nickel plated, acorn finial, w/bracket - $395.00
12" Bell marked "Seagrave" - $525.00
12" Bell marked "American La France", eagle finial - $675.00
12" Brass Bell with "Goddess of Liberty" finial - $1750.00

Belts

Patent leather belts for firemen were useful as well as decorative. Very common during the 1800s, leather belts featured sewn on lettering and came in several colors. Ordinarily, the company name and number were sewn on the belt. Some belts had a leather sheath to hold a spanner wrench, or a decorative metal hook that acted as a helmet hanger. Other belts had a strap with a spring to secure to a ladder while operating a nozzle. As an added feature, many belts had a leather slide loop that made the belt look pleasing to the eye.

Most belts had small inner buckles, and some had a decorative outer buckle. These buckles were made of metal and featured designs such as hose, fire apparatus, or a fireman's scramble. Along with the design, the company's number was usually embossed on the buckle. A belt with a decorative metal buckle is generally more desirable than a belt with a slide. Try to find a colorful belt with all of the sewn letters intact. Belts that have missing letters or have severely deteriorated leather should be avoided. It is normal to find some cracking of the leather and fading of colors on old belts.

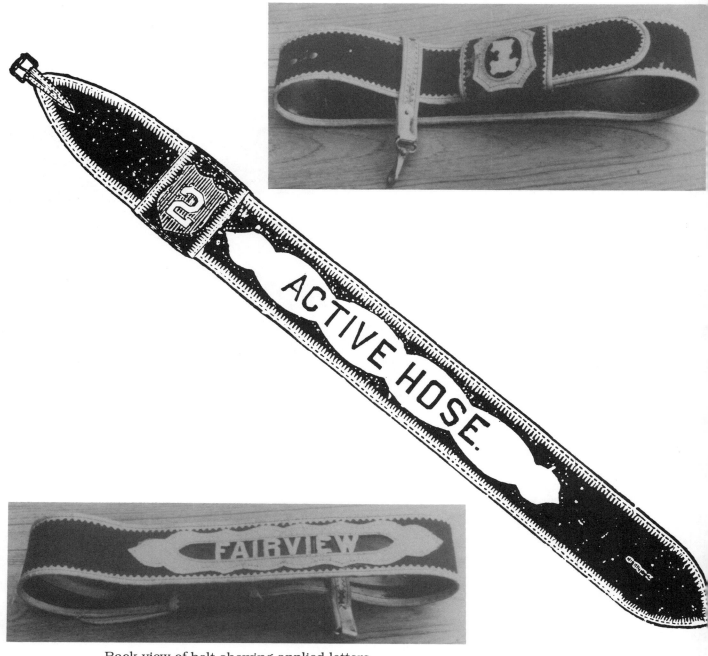

Back view of belt showing applied letters
& stitched applique, "FAIRVIEW"

Belts

BELTS.

FIG. 100.

Square Metal Clasps, when put on belts, same price as Round Clasps, dozen extra. They are mostly nickel-plated.

FIG. 101.

Fancy Stitched Belt, each $3.00.

FIG. 102.

FIG. 103.

Fancy colored Belts, bound . . . .
Fancy colors, stitched edge . . . .
Black bound Belts . . . .
Black Belts, stitched edge . . . .

Our Belts are all stitched with silk, and are made in a neat manner

Fancy stitched Belts

FIREMEN'S BELTS.

Our belts are made of fine quality patent leather, silk stitched, in any of the regulation colors. Unless otherwise specified the bound edge belt (Plate 264) will be sent.

Plate 264.

Bound Edge Belt.

Plate 264. Both edges bound with enamelled leather. Made in any color or combination of colors.
Price, each . . . .

Plate 265.

Full Stitched Belt.

Plate 265. Both edges stitched instead of being bound; otherwise same as regular bound edge belt.
Price, each . . . .

Plate 266.

Half Stitched Belt.

Plate 266. Stitched only the length of name panel.
Price, each . . . .

Plate 267.

Spanner Belts.

For carrying one or two spanners; made from heavy leather.
With one Spanner loop . . . . per doz.
" two " . . . . "

BELTS.

No. 137.

Black leather Service Belt, with Spanner Loop, ... per doz.,
137a. Black patent leather, 2 in. wide, plain panel, no letters,
137b. Colored . . . "
137c. Same as 137, black, lettered, . . . "
137d. " " colored, . . . "
137e. " " " black, lined edges, stitched 2¼ in. wide, "
137f. " " " colored, . . . "
137g. Black patent leather, fancy panel, edges bound and stitched, 2⅜ in. wide, . . . "
137. Colored patent leather, fancy panel, edges bound and stitched, 2⅜ in. wide, . . . "

No. 138.

PER DOZEN.

138. Black patent leather, fancy scroll panel scalloped edges, bound and stitched, 2½ inches wide, . . . "
138a. Colored patent leather, fancy scroll panel scalloped edges, bound and stitched, 2½ inches wide, . . . "

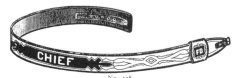

No. 138.

139. Colored Patent Leather, Extra Scroll Panel, Fancy Stitched, Scalloped Edges, 2½ in. wide, per doz., $50.00. For Leather Letters in excess of seven, 3 cents each. For Nickel or Silver Block Letters, 12 cents each. For Silvered or Gilt Gothic Letters, 15 cents each.

Belts

Leather Belt from Union Co. with [...] buckle.

Parade Belt, leather, black belt with white letters on a red background.

Leather Belt, Cumberland Hose [...] nickel buckle & letters.

Leather Belt from "The Hand in Hand Brigade".

Top - Leather Belt, Goodwill Brigade, Ph[...] delphia, PA, 1872
Middle - Leather Belt, Asst. Engineer G[...] will Brigade, 1872
Bottom - Leather Belt, Colwyn Brig[...] Colwyn, PA, 1894

Price Guide for Belts

(#2 Condition)
Leather Belt with slide and applied – $175.00
Leather, with stitched letters and slide - $125.00
Leather, with stitched letters and buckle - $175.00
Leather, 3 color, with metal letters and buckle - $250.00
Helmet hanger belt hook, nickel w/fireman & child - $50.00
Belt buckle, round brass buckle w/hose border & raised 2 in center - $50.00
Belt buckle, brass & German silver oval, w/steamer - $75.00

Books, Catalogs, Magazines & Journals

Books.

Any great collection begins with interest in the subject. One of the best ways to cultivate interest and increase knowledge on the subject is by doing research. By knowing the basic history of firefighting, a person can begin to understand and appreciate fire collectibles. Therefore it is a good idea to build a small library of fire related books and other sources of information. The books that are of greatest collectible value are early comprehensive firefighting history books with illustrations. Two fine examples include "Our Firemen" by Augustine Costello published in 1887 and "Reminiscenes of the Old Fire Laddies and Volunteer Fire Departments of New York and Brooklyn" dated 1885 by J.F Kernan. There are two books of later vintage that are very helpful to the collector. They are "Enjine! Enjine!" published in 1939 and "As You Pass By" published in 1952. Both books were written by Kenneth Dunshee and can be found with a little searching. An inexpensive reprint is available of "Enjine! Enjine!". The collector who has a special interest in firemarks should possess a copy of "Footprints of Assurance" by Alwin Bulau, published in 1953. There are hundreds of other books on the history of firefighting and various fire departments. Some books feature items from musuem collections such as "The Historical Collection of the Insurance Co. of North America" by M. J. McCosker, 1945. Not many books have been written specifically on fire collectibles. However, two informative books are available. The first book was "Firehouse Collectibles" by Mary Jane and James Piatti, published in 1979 and now in its second edition. The second book was "Firehouse Memorabilia" by Chuck Deluca, which was published in 1989.

Catalogs.

Catalogs are another excellent source of reference material. On the pages of these old catalogs are detailed illustrations of various firefighting equipment, uniforms, badges, alarm boxes and apparatus. Late 1800's catalogs are very scarce and are going up in value. A few reprints are available at a fraction of the price of an original catalog. It is interesting to note the prices of the items. Many price quotes applied to "by the dozen".

Magazines.

Magazines are another way to open a window to the past. Old magazines such as Fireman's Herald, Firemens Standard, Fire Engineering and Fireman feature articles and advertising of a bygone era of firefighting. On occasion, Harper's Weekly, Wide Awake Weekly and Pluck and Luck featured stories and colorfully illustrated covers about firefighting. Modern publications such as "Firehouse" are still providing insight into the profession of firefighting. Some editions feature articles on old apparatus and fire collectibles.

Journals.

Journals from fire departments provide a written record of day to day events. Fire runs, rescue runs, and activities around the station are logged in these books. Journals can be very helpful when compiling a local history of a small department. In addition, early examples of rules and regulations books for specific departments can be interesting to read and are also collectible.

Leave It To Beaver Book, 210 pgs. 1962 by Gomalco, Inc.

MAD Magazine, Dec. 1980 issue.

Books, Catalogs, Magazines & Journals

PRICE GUIDE TO BOOKS, CATALOGS, MAGAZINES & JOURNALS

Book Pricing.
"As You Pass By", by Kenneth H. Dunshee, 1952 - $45.00
"Enjine! Enjine!", by Kenneth H. Dunshee, 1939 - $75.00
Reprint of "Enjine! Enjine!" - $15.00
"Fires and Fighters", by John V. Morris, 1955 - $35.00
"Footprints of Assurance", by Alwin E. Bulau, 1953 - $60.00
"History of the American Steam Fire Engine", by W.T. King - $250.00
"Our Firemen-A History of the New York Fire Dept.-Volunteer and Paid", by A. Costello, 1887 - $275.00
"Reminiscences of the Old Fire Laddies and Volunteer Fire Departments of New York and Brooklyn,
        by J.F. Kernan, 1885 - $250.00
"The Historical Collection of the Insurance Co. of North America", by M.J. McCosker, 1945 - $35.00
"The Historical Collection of the Home Insurance Co.", 1945 - $65.00
"The Romance of Firefighting", by Robert S. Holzman, 1956 - $35.00
"Ye Olde Fire Laddies", by H. Asbury, 1930 - $65.00
"Heritage of Flames", by Donald Connan, 1975 - $40.00
"American Firemarks", by Insurance Co. of America, 1933 - $45.00
"100 Years of American Fire Fighting Apparatus", by Paul Dacosta, 1964 - $25.00
"The American Firehouse", by Rebacca Zurier, 1982. - $30.00
"Firefighters and Their Pets", by A. Downes, 1907 - $95.00
"Chicago's Awful Theatre Horror", by the survivors, 1904 - $45.00
"The Story of the Volunteer Fire Department of the City of New York", by George W. Sheldon, 1892 - $250.00
"Fire Department, Haverhill, MA, Complete History", hardcover, 1897 - $85.00
"History of the Brooklyn, New York Fire Department", leather bound, 1892 - $275.00

Childrens Books.
"The Young Fireman of Lakeville", 1909 - $30.00
"Five Little Firemen", 1948 - $15.00
Big Little Book, "Our Gang Adventures", 1948 - $30.00
"The Book of Model Fire Engines", by Grossett & Dunlop, has punchout &
        assemble fire station & fire trucks, 1951 - $50.00
"Leave It To Beaver" Book, 210 pgs., 1962 by Gomalco, Inc. – $15.00

Catalog Pricing.
Henry K. Barnes, Fire Department Supplies, Boston, Mass., 1895 - $225.00
Fred J. Miller, Fire Apparatus and Fire Department supplies, New York, 1884 - $275.00
D. A. Woodhouse M'F'G Co. Manufacturers of Fire Department Supplies, 1888-89 - $225.00
Catalogue of Firemens Uniforms & Equipment of Henderson & Co. - $225.00
Modern Firefighting Equipment, American LaFrance & Foamite Corp., 1929 - $75.00
Firemen's Uniforms, Browning King & Co. - $75.00
S.W. Reese Badge Co. Catalog, 1913 - $85.00
Darley Municipal Fire Protection & Police Supply, 1928 - $50.00

Magazine Pricing.
The Fire Service Review, Vol. 1, #4, 1894 - $100.00
Fire Engineering Magazine, Oct,. 1928 - $25.00
Firehouse Magazine, Charter issue, Sept./Oct., 1976 - $30.00
Fireman's Herald - $65.00-75.00
MAD Magazine, December 1980 issue – $10.00
Pluck & Luck - $35.00
Wide Awake Weekly - $30.00
Fire Deparment Journal, circa 1890 - $50.00-75.00
Fire Department Rules & Regulations, 1900 - $35.00-45.00

Buckets

Before the advent of municipal water systems and motorized fire pumpers, the best way to get water from its source to the fire was by means of buckets and bucket brigades. As early as 1686, many houses in New York City were required to have one bucket hung near the front door. When the cry of "fire" was heard, citizens would throw out their buckets so other citizens and firemen could easily pick them up. There were two lines to the bucket brigade. The first line passed filled buckets from the cistern or water supply to the fire. A cistern is a tank that catches and stores the rainwater. The second line returned the empty buckets for refilling. Each bucket held 2 1/2 to 3 gallons of water, and weighed 25 to 30 pounds when full. Leather proved to be a superior material to wood for durability in the construction of fire buckets. Throughout the 1700's and early 1800's hand sewn leather buckets were the standard.

About 1820, riveted buckets were introduced. These riveted buckets were more durable but unfortunately the leather was still susceptible to rot. The vulcanization of rubber led to the use of rubber fire buckets as early as the 1840's.

Fire buckets usually had the owner's name, initials, or number painted in oil on them. Some buckets had coats-of-arms or elaborately painted portraits as part of their identification. This was required so owners could claim their buckets after a fire.

Buckets were also constructed of cork or metal. Metal fire buckets were used mainly in commercial establishments. These buckets usually have rounded or pointed bottoms. They were made this way to increase capacity and to discourage the use as a mop bucket. Metal fire buckets could be filled with water, a calcium chloride solution or sand.

Original leather fire buckets are the most valuable, especially those that can be documented and are lavishly illustrated. A leather fire bucket painted by a famous artist or a bucket with a portrait of a famous person would be highly sought after.

When examining leather fire buckets for purchase, check to see if the handle has been repaired or replaced. Many buckets had leather encased, rope handles. Craquelure (crack paint) and paint loss can diminish the value of a fire bucket. Note the condition of the leather and if the bucket has been repainted. A faded design may be restored by a qualified artist. Remember, the better the condition and the more elaborate the decoration on the bucket, the greater is its value.

nd painted leather fire bucket arked "City Fire Society", Sam ilnwath 1822", depicting a night ene of fireman battling a build- g fire, original paint, #3 condi- n.

Leather fire bucket, 11" tall, hand painted image of a Native American with bow and arrows. Columbia Southwick from Connecticut – circa 1806.

FIRE BUCKETS.

Leather, plain, per dozen . .
Leather, painted   "   . .
Rubber, Flexible, with stiffened bottoms, the best bucket now made, per dozen . . . .
Heavy Rubber, per dozen.
Papier Mache ; these are something new in Fire Buckets, are light and strong ; any color, per dozen . . . .

Rubber.
FIG. 70.

Iron.
FIG. 71.

GALVANIZED IRON BUCKETS.

Iron, 7 quart, per dozen . . . .
  " 10 "   "   . . . .
  " 14 "   "   . . . .
  "   7 " with covers, per dozen . . . .
  " 10 "   "   . . . .
  " 14 "   "   " . . . .

Buckets

Leather Fire Bucket, painted green with gold letters.

Leather Bucket, painted red with gold lettering.

Leather Fire Bucket, finely decorated with figure of mercury blowing a trumpet, marked J. Pierce, Active 1806, 12 3/4" Tall.

Standard Type Metal Fire Bucket, painted red.

19th Century Fireman's Memorial Bucket. Black with gold lettering, (Restored).

Leather Fire Bucket, painted red with gold stripes, note: iron reinforcing bands around top & bottom.

Buckets

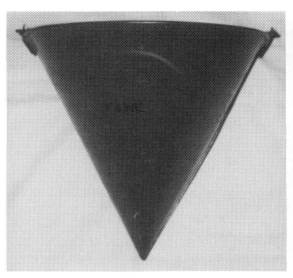

Conical Metal Fire Bucket, painted red.

Left - Leather Fire Bucket, painted green with gold lettering & flourishes.
Center - English Fire Bucket, leather with riveted seams.
Right - Leather Fire Bucket, originally painted gold.
All three buckets have replacement handles.

Leather Fire Bucket reproduction by Cairns, 1950's.

Leather Fire Bucket, finely decorated, green with gold trim, E. W. Mitchell, 1827.

Buckets

PRICE GUIDE FOR BUCKETS

19th Century Fireman's Memorial Bucket – $800.00
Fire bucket, leather, painted black from hook`& ladder-no markings - $250.00-275.00
Fire bucket, leather, painted in two colors w/name - $500.00-600.00
Leather w/name, fire Co.-some flourishment - $800.00-1650.00
Leather w/name, fire Co. & date-elaborately decorated with emblem or scene - $2750.00-5500.00
Rubber fire bucket - $175.00
Fiber compostion fire bucket, wire bail w/wood handle, painted red, 1880's - $135.00
Metal fire bucket, painted red w/fire in black - $45.00
Leather fire bucket w/riveted seams, painted red - $375.00
English fire bucket, leather, painted red with black bands & coat of arms - $425.00
Reproduction fire bucket, brown leather w/gold American eagle & red, white & blue shield,
    made by Cairns, 1950's - $125.00
Leather fire bucket, clasped hands, green with gold trim, marked E.W. Mitchell, 1827 - $12,000.00
Finely painted leather bucket with figure of Mercury blowing a trumpet,
    "J.Pierce Active 1806", 12 3/4" tall - $35,000.00
Leather bucket, red with gold lettering, marked "Torrent Six Roxbury, 1829" - $1500.00
Pair of decorated fire buckets with gold lettering on red background "South Potter" – $3500.00
Hand painted leather fire bucket marked "City Fire Society, Sam Asilnwath 1822" – $6500.00
Hand painted leather fire bucket with a lavishly painted fire scene, marked "William Lovejoy,
    Enterprise Fire Club" – $8500.00
Leather fire bucket with sewn seems, marked "C. Borden 1829" – $1500.00
Leather fire bucket with hand painted eagle, marked "J.R. Hoar Warren, R.I." – $7500.00
Leather fire bucket, 11" tall, hand painted image of a Native American with
    bow and arrows. Columbia Southwick from Connecticut, circa 1806 – $3000.00

Leather fire bucket with sewn seams, marked "C. Borden 1829".

Pair of decorated fire buckets with gold lettering on red background "South Potter".

Leather fire bucket with hand painted eagle, marked "J.R. Hoar Warren, R.I."

Hand painted leather fire bucket with a lavishly painted fire scene, marked "William Lovejoy, Enterprise Fire Club".

Buttons & Pins

Buttons.

Buttons have been used for centuries. Examples of primitive buttons have been found in ancient tombs. Firemen's uniforms have traditionally been embellished with buttons in a gold or silver finish. Some of the finest quality buttons ever made were 19th Century gilt buttons. These buttons were made of brass with a thin wash of gold.

Buttons were used on caps, uniform shirts and jackets. Gleaming gold or silver buttons sewn on a dark blue, dress uniform creates a very professional appearance. The use of special buttons for firemen's uniforms continues to this day.

Most fire department buttons are marked F.D. and some have the city's name on them. Unusual buttons feature designs of helmets, hydrants or fire apparatus. Typically, firefighters, sergeants, lieutenants, and captains had silver buttons on their uniforms. Higher ranking officers such as Deputy Chiefs and Chiefs would have gold buttons.

Many buttons were stamped with a manufacturer on the reverse side of the button. These are called back marks.

Fire Department buttons are relatively plentiful and inexpensive. Many button designs have not changed over the years, and are still being used on present day uniforms.

Celluloid buttons with pin backs are another area of button collecting. This type of button is normally associated with political buttons. However, many collectible buttons with a firemanic theme have been produced since the early 1900's. Numerous buttons were issued for conventions, and depict firemen, apparatus and fire scenes.

Pins.

Fire Department pins are another related area of collecting. Pins are usually round and are used as collar insignias or cap badges. Most pins are silver or gold finished and some feature an enameled background.

Firefighter pins show a helmet, trumpet, ladder, axe, nozzle, and pike pole in a grouped design. This design is referred to as a firemen's scramble. Pins can indicate rank and are worn on the shirt collar and cap. One trumpet or bugle for lieutenant, two for captain, Five bugles indicates a rank of chief.

Often, when a member of the fire service retires, the pins and badges of various ranks the member held are collected. These items are mounted on a plaque and presented to the member as an honorary memento.

Buttons & Pins

BADGE CENTERS & INSIGNIA

A2963

A2988

A2991

Please be sure to specify background color on all enamel centers when ordering. Available in red, white or blue enamel.

A2994

A2997

A3025

A3507

A3535

A3028

A2965

A2990

A2993

A2996

A2999

A3027

A3536

A3533

A3030

A2964

A2989

A2992

A2995

A2998

A3026

A3537

A3534

A3029

A2547
w/app. A2905

A2547
w/app. A2906

A2547
w/app. A2907

A2547
w/app. A2908

A2547
w/app. A2909-2

A2547
w/app. A2909

A2547 series cannot be used as badge centers. For use as cap badges or collar insignia only.

A3061

A3317

A3316

A3375

A3061 through A3378. Please be sure to specify color choice for enamel background of rim.
Available only with lettering shown. Takes 15/16" center. Specify choice of color for enamel background of center also.

24   A3376

A3548

A3377

A3378

Original Catalog Page

75

Buttons & Pins

Be sure to specify titles and enamel color desired for centers

A2868

A2869

A2870

A2882

A2883

A2861

A2862

A2866

A2864

A2860

A4279

A2863

A2867

A2865

A2905

A2906

A2907

A2908

A2909-2

A2909

A2871

A4280

A2873

A2874

A2875

A2876

Smooth Background Fire Horn badge centers or insignia available—plain only—
Corresponding enameled styles shown on page 24.

A3574

A2872

A3615

A3575

A3614

A3613

Embossed background fire horn badge centers or insignia.

27

Buttons & Pins

BLACKINTON — America's largest selection of appropriate badge centers and insignia.

A2889   A2955   A2961   B385   A2956   A2960

A2890
Avail with #'s 1, 2, 3

A2940   A2957   A2941   A2891   A4216

A2891A

A2884   A2885   A2886   A2939   A4156

A3715

A2888B   A2888A   A2888   A2484
Smooth Bkg.

A2327

A2887
Embossed Bkdg

11549D   A4261D   A4261Q

A4215

11549A   A4261A   B328   A4261B   A4261L   11549G   A4261G   B327   11549C   A4261C   B324

11549E   A4261E   B326   11549F   A4261F   B325   11549H   A4261H   A4261M

11549J   A4261J   A4261N   11549K   A4261K   A4261P   A4218   A4218A   A4218B

B1041

Lettering: Years service is in
die may have enamel bkg.
Center may be stenciled
with any number.

34

Original Catalog Page

Buttons & Pins

COLLAR INSIGNIA.

(All illustrations on this page are actual size.)

Plate 284.	Plate 285.	Plate 286.
Style No. 167.	Style No. 168.	Style No. 169.
Chief Engineer.	1st Assistant Chief.	2nd Assistant Chief.
Nickel......	Nickel......	Nickel......
Gilt.........	Gilt.........	Gilt.........

FOR
ENGINE
OR
HOSE
COMPANY.

Plate 287.	Plate 288.
Style No. 170.	Style No. 171.
Nickel......	Nickel......
Gilt.........	Gilt.........

FOR
HOOK
AND
LADDER
COMPANY.

Plate 289.	Plate 290.
Style No. 172.	Style No. 173.
Nickel......	Nickel......
Gilt.........	Gilt.........

Buttons.

Regulation Fire Buttons.   F. D. Buttons.

Assorted Celluloid Buttons

Buttons & Pins

Fire Dept. Button, Dayton.

Fire Dept. Button, New York City.

Button from Los Angeles featuring a steamer.

Standard Types of Buttons.

Left - Button from a Chief's uniform.
Right - Button from a Captain's uniform.

Celluloid Button with pin back, fireman's celebration.

PRICE GUIDE FOR BUTTON & PINS

Plain button with letters F.D. - $1.00-3.00
Nickel plated button w/F.D. name & design - $5.00-10.00
Gilt button w/hook & ladder design & #1 - $15.00
Button with firemen & torch, circa 1830's - $40.00
Button from Vigilante Fire Hose Co. with wood hydrant, hose , and eye, 1835 - $50.00
Celluloid button with color illustration & pin back - $20.00-45.00
Firemen's Celebration pin - $17.50
Fire department pins (various insignias) - $15.00-18.00 each

Capes

One of the earliest forms of protective clothing for a fireman was a cape. Capes were worn over the shoulders to protect the men from hot embers and water. The first capes worn in the United States were by the men of Assistance Fire Company of Philadelphia in 1794. These first capes were made of oyl cloth. Oyl cloth or oil cloth, was a fabric treated with oil, clay and pigments to make it waterproof. Later, canvas was used instead of oyl cloth and was coated with at least three layers of paint for added protection. The cape was painted with the company's name, colors and the founding date. Many capes had beautiful illustrations done by local artists. Capes are extremely rare and are found mainly in large museum collections.

Capes

Cape of Friendship Fire Company, painted oyl cloth.

Oyl Cloth Cape.

Capes

Cape from Philadelphia Fire Company, painted oyl cloth.

PRICE GUIDE FOR CAPES

Extremely Rare - $4000.00-6000.00
Finely Illustrated Cape - $12,000.00 +

Cards

Trade cards.

     The trade card boom began in 1876. Trade cards were a form of advertising in an era devoid of radio and television. Printed by the thousands, trade cards touted new products of the industrial revolution. Most featured inexpensive color lithography and some cards were die cut to follow the outline of the illustration. Other unique cards produced were mechanical cards and metamorphic cards. Mechanical cards have moving parts usually activated by tabs. Metamorphic cards unfold to expose a dramatic change in the illustration. Condition of a trade card affects value. Bends, stains or cards that have been trimmed, all detract from the price.

Postcards.

     During the turn of the century, postcards were popular in Europe. In 1906, the craze spread to the United States. An astounding 968 million postcards were sold in the U. S. during 1913. This was the heyday of the postcard.

     After World War I, the use of the postcard dwindled. However, during the 1960's, the public developed a new interest in postcards. Literally thousands of postcards have been produced with fire related themes. Cards from the early 1900's are the most desirable, especially mechanicals.

1967 Postcard of The Steam Fire Engine "Abe Lincoln"

Number 13 of 16 pictures of "Our Fire Department", informational cards, 10" x 13" issued in 1954.

Pair of Black & White Postcards, featuring apparatus.

Cards

Postcard of a 1931 American LaFrance Rescue Squad.

ostcard of a Hand Pumper, presented by George Washington.

PRICE GUIDE FOR CARDS

Trade Card Pricing.
"The Fireman" set of six humorous color cards by Cosak & Clarke, 1887 - $175.00
Player cigarettes set of 50 - $150.00
"Firefighters" set of 64, Bowman Gum Co. - $95.00

Postcards Pricing.
Steamer racing to a fire, w/3 white horses, color - $15.00
Firehouse & apparatus, Hastings, NE, in color - $15.00
Fireboat New Yorker, FDNY color - $15.00
Hook & ladder Co. going to an alarm, FDNY color - $25.00
Chemical engine 16 responding, FDNY color - $25.00
Auto Chemical Co. #1, New Bedford, MA, black & white - $15.00
Hand pumper presented by George Washington - $12.00
1967 postcard of the steam fire engine "Abe Lincoln" - $15.00
Black & white postcard featuring apparatus - $10.00-15.00

Certificates

During the 1800's, fire companies issued various types of certificates. If a fireman was an active member of a fire company, he would have been issued a membership certificate. Many years later, after serving his required time in the volunteer fire company, the member would become exempt. At this time, an exemption certificate would be issued. One of the perks of being exempt was that the member did not have to serve at jury duty. In certain instances, honorary certificates were presented to individuals who helped the fire company.

Many certificates were made with beautiful color lithographs of fire equipment and fire scenes. Some examples of certificates were done by famous print makers such as Currier & Ives, and featured hand tinting.

Generally, the older more elaborate and colorful the design, the greater the value of the certificate. An unissued certificate is not as desirable as an issued one. As with any paper collectible, rips, folds, stains, discoloration and trimming, all detract from overall value.

Certificate of the Firemen's Protective Association of Cincinatti, OH.

Presentation Certificate, full color lithograph, 1854, 14 1/2" x 19 1/2".

PRICE GUIDE FOR CERTIFICATES

Plain Certificate with no design - $65.00-95.00
Pre-1900 with design and hand coloring - $325.00-575.00
Post 1900 with color lithography - $150.00-275.00
Certificate from New York Volunteer Fire Company with Neptune, 1864 - $350.00
Philadelphia Assoc. for the Relief of Disabled Firemen. with colorful fire scene, hand engines
     & two firemen in parade hats with play pipes, 1863 - $550.00
Detroit Fireman's Fund Assoc., 1922 - $175.00
Fireman's Protective Assoc. of Cincinatti, OH, 1901 - $225.00
Fire Department Certificate with city seal, 1891 - $165.00
Presentation Certificate, full color lithograph, 1854, 14 1/2" x 19 1/2" - $395.00
Membership Certificate by Currier & Ives, pictured on page 150 - $450.00-500.00
Fireman's Honorable Discharge Certificate, pictured on page 150 - $650.00

Engine Builder's Nameplates

Steam fire engines were operated and cared for by firemen who had pride in their "masheens". When a piece of fire apparatus was ready to be replaced, the engine builder's nameplate was removed and kept as a memento. This practice is still being done today.

Engine builder's nameplates were typically made of brass and some were plated with silver or chromium. On the nameplate, the manufacturer's name is found along with the number. Some examples of nameplates include for whom the engine was built.

Nameplates from steamers are the most desirable. Two famous makers of steam fire engines were the Amoskeag Steam Fire Engine Company of Manchester, New Hampshire and The LaFrance Fire Engine Company of Elmira, New York.

Below is a list of other fire apparatus builders, most of whom have long since disappeared into history:

Ahrens-Fox
Buffalo
Four Wheel Drive
Hahn
Howe
Kissel
Mack
Pirsch
Sanford
Seagrave
White
Clapp & Jones
Silsby

American LaFrance Fire Engine Co.
Builder's Plate.

PRICE GUIDE FOR ENGINE BUILDER'S NAMEPLATES

Hand Pumper Builders Plate - $750.00 +
Steam Fire Engine Builders Plate - $500.00-600.00
Motorized Fire Engine Builders Plate - $35.00-125.00

Engine Lamps

During the 1800's, fire apparatus were being outfitted with lamps to light the way to a night fire. Early engine lamps were made of tin with mica windows. By about 1840, engine lamps were being made quite large and with ornamentation. Lamps of this era were typically brass and some were silver plated. Glass panels were used, and many were engraved with the fire company's name and number. A variety of colors of glass were available for lamps. Colors included red, green, blue, clear or a split panel option of two colors could be ordered. Some lamps had finials in the shape of eagles, firemen or acorns. Very desirable are main engine lamps and lamps mounted to a wooden pole, known as pole lamps.

Six-sided engine lamp; silver plated with red & blue glass panels and etched floral designs. Triumph 1 made by DeVoursney & Bros., 18" tall.

Six-sided engine lamp, beautifully etched red and blue glass panels, nickel plated.

Engine Lamps

PATENT
Swinging Reflecting Signal.

OROIDE or BRASS. Vermillion Painted Body.
Large size, ... each, $26.00
Small size, ... " 21.00
SILVER or NICKEL, Vermillion Painted Body.
Large size, ... each, $30.00
Small size, ... " 23.00

Hexagon Signal Lamps.
Plate 189.
Finished in heavy nickel plate
or polished brass.

8½ inch swing.

. . . .

Boiler Side Lamps.
Plate 190.
Finished in heavy nickel plate
or polished brass. Ruby glass
engraved and lettered; glasses
4½ inches diameter.
Price . . . .

Plate 189.

Six Sided Engine Lamp, w/
red, blue & white panels &
etched floral designs, made
by De Voursney & Bros.,
18" Tall

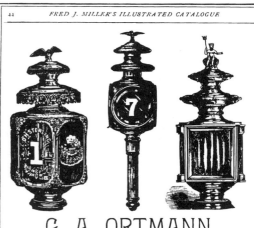

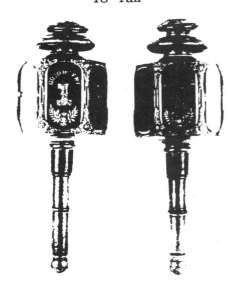

Pair of Engine Side Lamps,
made by De Voursney Bros., 9
Broome Street, New York, late
19th century, each with two
blue, one red and clear etched
glass panels, the red panels
inscribed "Good Intent", used
Pottsville, Penn., possibly from
Amoskeag Steamer, the first
purchased July, 1883,
19 1/2" Tall.

Engine Lamps

Engine Side
Lamp, nickel
plated, 19" tall,
made by De
Voursney & Bros.

Brass Engine Lamp,
Essex Company, red
glass, eagle finial,
1840's.

Engine Lamp w/3
round glass pan-
els, front is
"Protector 17" red
panel, side is blue
"Protector 17"
and other side
panel is clear
with "17" and
floral designs.
24" tall.

Brass Side
Lamp from a
hand operated
engine, red
glass with
etched "3",
21" tall.

Brass Lamp from a hose
cart, w/red and clear
glass.

Engine Lamps

PRICE GUIDE FOR ENGINE LAMPS

Ornate, brass main engine lamp w/ colored & etched glass panels from early apparatus - $2750.00-3750.00

Engine lamp, "Protector 17", red, blue & clear glass, etched with floral designs, 24" tall - $2950.00

Lamp from a steamer, nickel plated, 17" high w/clear beveled glass panels w/etched steamer
 & floral design, eagle finial - $2250.00

Hose wagon side lamps, nickel plated, ruby glass with the letters "Eagle" & etched floral designs,
 made by Devournsney Brothers - $4250.00 pair

Early pole lamp made of tin & decorated - $2750.00

Set of 3, hose carriage lamps, 1 main light & 2 side lights, brass with etched colored glass panels &
 eagle finials - $5500.00 set

Brass side lamp from a hand operated engine, red glass with etched 3, 21" tall - $1750.00 pair

Engine lamp, six sided, red, blue & white panels with etched floral designs, eagle finial, "McQuoid 3",
 made by Devoursney & Brothers, 18" tall - $25000.00

Engine side lamp, nickel plated, made Devoursney & Bros., 19" tall - $2000.00 pair

Pair of engine side lamps, "Good Intent 1", made by Devoursney & Bros.,
 19 1/2" tall - $3000.00 pair

Six-sided engine lamp; silver plated with red & blue glass panels, Triumph I made by
 DeVoursney & Bros., 18" tall – $2500.00

Six-sided engine lamp, nickel plated with red and blue glass panels – $2750.00

Extinguisher, Fire

During the late 1800's, soda-acid extinguishers were being developed. Basically, this form of extinguisher was comprised of a cylinder containing a soda solution and a glass bottle of acid. One type of extinguisher when inverted, allowed a glass bottle to be released from a holder. When the glass bottle was broken, the acid would mix with the soda and a chemical reaction would occur. A buildup of pressure would expel the solution and could be used to extinguish a fire.

Inverting type soda-acid extinguishers were made with copper shells held together with rivets until about 1942. At that time, drawn brass shells replaced the copper riveted ones.

In 1969 the manufacturing of all soda-acid extinguishers was discontinued in the United States. Many of these extinguishers, when improperly tested or maintained would explode when used. The collector should keep in mind the hazards relating to these extinguishers and should never attempt to invert or discharge a full and complete soda-acid extinguisher.

Back in the early 1900's, tin tube extinguishers filled with a dry chemical such as sodium bicarbonate were becoming popular. Tin tubes came in a variety of sizes and were meant to be hung from a hook. When the user pulled the tin tube, the top would come off. The contents of the tube could then be shaken out onto the fire. Many tin tubes featured colorful designs and fancy lettering.

In 1905, Pyrene Manufacturing Co. of Newark, New Jersey introduced the first model of fire extinguisher with a single action pump. This particular model used carbon tetrachloride as the extinguishing agent. If you find an extinguisher filled with carbon tet., be aware that the vapors of CCL4 are toxic and if applied to a fire will produce deadly phosgene gas. By the mid 1960's, most jurisdictions banned the use of these types of extinguishers.

During World War I, the first carbon dioxide extinguishers were produced and in 1917, the foam extinguisher was developed. The foam extinguisher worked in a similar fashion as the soda-acid extinguisher and was used until the 1950's.

The year was 1928 when the first dry-chemical, cartridge operated extinguisher was invented. However, it wasn't until 1953 that the first stored pressure, multipurpose dry-chemical extinguisher was introduced.

Stored pressure, water type extinguishers were also available and were popular from the 1940's through the 1970's. These types of extinguishers were typically made in brass or stainless steel.

The Halon 1301 extinguisher was first introduced in 1954 and the Halon 1211 extinguisher in 1973.

The field of collecting fire extinguishers is very large. Many collectors seek out early models of various manufacturers. Other collectors look for colorful tin tubes or soda-acid extinguishers made with copper.

Sizes of extinguishers range from a few inches long to the gigantic contraptions found on chemical engines or wheeled units. Pony sized copper or brass extinguishers are becoming harder to find and are quite collectible.

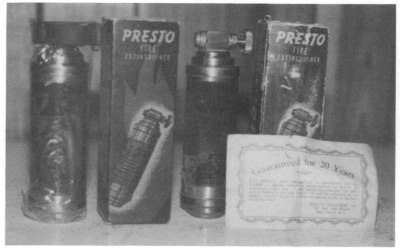

Miniature Presto fire extinguishers
with original packaging.

EXO fire extinguisher
liquid, 1 quart can.

Extinguisher, Fire

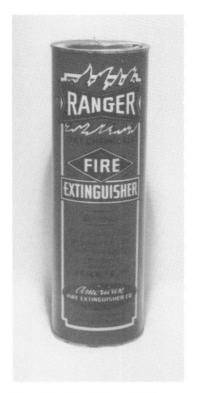

Ranger Fire Extinguisher.

Fire Dust Dry Chemical Extinguisher Tin.

Left - Instantaneous Fire
Extinguisher.
Right - Formagas Fire
Extinguisher.
Right - Liberty Fire
Extinguisher.

Hanks Guaranteed
Fire Extinguisher,
fiber tube.

Phoenix Fire
Extinguisher.

Hero Fire Extinguisher,
5" tall.

Extinguisher, Fire

Manville Fire Extinguisher.

Security Fire Extinguisher, tin tube with paper label.

Shur-ex, Bullet Shaped Extinguisher, designed to be mounted on an automobile.

Quick Aid Fire Extinguisher, brass with maroon painted bracket.

Fire Gun, brass, 1 1/2 quart fire extinguisher, made by American LaFrance Foamite Corporation.

Fyr Man Fire Extinguisher, black with orange label, fore runner to the Fyr-Fyter.

Extinguisher, Fire

Brass Presto
Fire Extin-
guisher with
red label,
4" long.

1-2-3 Fire Extin-
guisher, chro-
mium plated,
4" tall.

Fyr-Fyter Hand
Extinguisher

Gigantic 5 gallon Copper
"Foamite" Soda-Acid Extinguisher. When full this extinguisher was extremely
heavy and hard to move
quickly.

Security Presto
dry chemical
extinguisher,
2 1/2 pound,
Hudson Mfg.
Co.

2 Presto "C B" Fire Extinguishers

Extinguisher, Fire

Buffalo and Junior Buffalo, copper, soda-acid fire extinguishers

Empire Extinguisher, copper, bi-carbonate, 2½ gallon.

Valex Chemical Fire Extinguis[

PRICE GUIDE TO FIRE EXTINGUISHERS

2½ gallon copper, soda-acid extinguisher - $65.00-125.00
5 gallon copper, "Foamite" extinguisher - $325.00
Copper, pony sized extinguisher - $150.00
Brass, pump type carbon tet. with original bracket - $25.00
Miniature "Presto" fire extinguisher, brass with bracket & original box - $25.00 each
Tin tube fire extinguisher - $40.00-100.00
Tin tube "Ranger" fire extinguisher - $35.00
Hero extinguisher - $25.00
Cardboard tube extinguisher - $25.00-30.00
Indian tank, brass - $125.00
Brass, ceiling mount extinguisher, "Stop-Fire" with sprinkler head & pressure guage - $125.00
Empire extinguisher, copper, bi-carbonate, 2½ gallon - $65.00
Security Presto dry chemical extinguisher, 2½ pound, Hudson Mfg. Co. - $85
EXO fire extinguisher liquid, 1 quart can – $35.00

Firemarks

Early fire brigades were formed by insurance companies to fight fires only on insured houses. These insurance companies needed a method to identify their policy holders homes. Firemarks were plates of identification developed exclusively for this purpose. Usually affixed to the front of the dwelling about half way up, the firemark was readily visible from the street.

The first firemark in America was issued in 1752 by the Philadelphia Contributionship for the Insurance of Houses from Loss by Fire. This design is known as the Hand-in-Hand, and was cast in lead.

Some other famous American firemarks include:

Green Tree - Mutual Assurance Company for Insuring Houses from Loss by Fire (1784).
Eagle In Flight - Insurance Company of North America (1796).
Clasped Hands - Baltimore Equitable Society (1792).
FA - Hydrant & Hose - Fire Association of Philadelphia (1817).

Many different materials were used for firemarks. Examples include: cast iron, lead, copper, brass, zinc, tin, wood and terra cotta.

The use of firemarks began to fade in the U.S. around 1870. This was due to the rise of many paid fire departments.

Hundreds of different designs of firemarks have been documented. Typical shapes include: squares, rectangles, ovals, circles and shields. Most any firemark has become scarce and is collectible. Many firemarks are being reproduced in cast iron. Reproduction firemarks usually have a rougher finish and fresh paint.

The collecting of firemarks is a specialized field of its own. For more information, please read "Footprints of Assurance" by Alwin E. Bulau, published in 1953. There is also a club known as "The Firemarks Circle of the Americas", that one can join.

Firemarks

Fireman's Fund Insurance Company,
San Francisco, CA, 1863.

Firemark, United Firemen's Insurance Co. of Philadelphia,
cast iron, issued 1860.

Firemark The Green Tree-Mutual
Assurance Co., oval style, 1810.

Firemark, Hand in Hand, Philadelphia
Contributionship, cast iron, 1857.

Firemarks

Firemark Hydrant & Hose, Fire
Association of Philadelphia, cast
iron, 1863.

Firemark The Green Tree, Mutual
Assurance Co., lead w/wood shield,
1803.

Tin Firemark, Guardian Insurance,
English.

Firemark Display

Firemarks

PRICE GUIDE FOR FIREMARKS

Mutual Assurance, lead tree with wood shield - $165.00
Philadelphia Contributionship, joined hands in lead with wood shield - $225.00
Fire Association of Philadelphia, cast iron hydrant & hose - $165.00
Firemen's Insurance Co., cast iron with hand pumper - $165.00
United Firemans Insurance Co., cast iron with steamer - $165.00
Plain tin firemark - $100.00-125.00
Guardian Assurance Co., copper, English - $135.00
Hope Mutual, zinc with anchor design - $125.00
Baltimore Equitable Society, cast iron, clasped hands - $225.00
Firemans Fund Insurance Co., San Francisco, CA, 1863 - $200.00
Firehouse chair. Carved hardwood, showing axes, trumpets, helmet and hoses, with
    leather upholstery – $1500.00
Firehouse traffic signal – $500.00

ODDITIES

Firehouse chair. Carved hardwood, showing axes, trumpets, helmet and hoses, with leather upholstery.

Firehouse traffic signal.

Glass Fire Grenades & Extinguisher Bottles

Glass fire grenades.

In 1863, Alanson Crane was granted the first American patent for a fire grenade. Around 1870, glass fire grenades came into popular use in the United States. Fire grenades were bottles filled with carbon tetrachloride or salt solution that was intended to be thrown into a fire. When the grenade hit the fire, it would break and release its contents to extinguish the fire.

Collectors are skeptical if these fire grenades had any merit and if they really worked. In an era where portable fire extinguishers were unheard of, the fire grenade did provide a minimum amount of extinguishing capability. However, many buyers were lulled into a false sense of security. It would be foolish to believe these grenades could extinguish anything other than a small fire. Millions were sold in a complete range of colors to match any decor.

Typically, fire grenades were spherical in shape and had a short neck. Many grenades were sealed with a cork and cement. The cement would prevent liquid from escaping in the event the cork shrank. As an added protection, some grenades had a foil seal over the cork. On the neck of many grenades, a wire loop can be found. The wire loop was used to hang a grenade from a nail or hook on a wall. Some manufacturers sold two or three fire grenades together in a wire basket.

Between 1900 and 1920, fire grenades resembling light bulbs could be purchased with a special bracket. This bracket had a spring device and a fusible link. When the fusible link melted, the spring would cause a metal arm to shatter the grenade and release its contents into the fire. Fire grenades of this era could be ordered in a metal case, such as the Shur-Stop kit which contained six grenades. Another popular grenade was the Red Comet.

Probably the most famous manufacturer of fire grenades was the Harden Hand Fire Extinguisher Company of Chicago. Harden's grenades were made in 1 1/2 pints and 1 quart sizes. These grenades featured an embossed star with vertical ribs or a diamond quilted pattern. Early examples were made with a footed base. Glass color was usually light blue or cobalt blue. Harden's grenades are the most common of known types of fire grenades.

A rare Harden's grenade is the Harden's Improved Fire Extinguisher Hand Grenade Nest System patent date of 1889. This grenade was made in three separate sections and was held together with wire. One section was clear glass, the second section was amber and the third section was cobalt blue.

Hayward was another large producer of fire grenades. Working out of New York, Hayward's Hand Fire Grenade was produced in several colors. Colors produced were blue, green, amber and smoke. Another version, Hayward's Hand Grenade Fire Extinguisher, was made in a different glass pattern.

Babcock made a fire grenade called the Babcock Hand Grenade Non-freezing. Grenades came in blue, green, clear and amber colored glass. The company was later sold to American LaFrance.

Barnum made fire grenades including the Diamond brand. Diamond grenades were made in a three sided and a four sided version. These grenades are clear and have a patent date of 1869.

Fire grenades were also made for use on railroad cars. One such grenade has the markings, C & NW Ry, indicating it was used by the Chicago & Northwestern Railway.

A large number of other manufacturers are known. Here are some of the more famous and desirable fire grenades to collect:

    American Fire Extinguisher - clear glass
    Boger Fire Extinguisher - clear glass
    California Fire Extinguisher - amber glass with embossed bear
    Eddison's Electric Fire Exterminator - clear glass, very rare
    Globe Fire Grenade
    Harkness Fire Destroyer - blue glass
    Hazelton's High Pressure Chemical Fire Keg - amber glass
    Healy's Fire Grenade
    HSN Fire Grenade - amber
    PSN Fire grenade - dark brown
    Kalamazoo Automatic & Hand Fire Extinguisher - cobalt blue
    Little Giant - clear glass with firecracker
    Rockford Kalamazoo Automatic & Hand Fire Extinguisher - blue
    Magic Fire
    Y-Burn Winner - blue glass, egg shaped

Fire extinguisher bottles.

Fire extinguisher bottles are similar to grenades in that they were made of glass and were meant to extinguish fires. Grenades were designed to be thrown and broken. Many extinguisher bottles were filled with a dry chemical that could be shaken out onto a fire. Fire extinguisher bottles were mounted on early automobiles in case of engine fires.

Glass Fire Grenades & Extinguisher Bottles

A popular extinguisher bottle to collect is marked the Dri Gas Fire Extinguisher Chattanooga, Tenn.. This clear, 13" bottle has a diamond quilted pattern and was filled with a sandy colored, dry chemical. The directions on the bottle states: Throw contents forcibly at the base of the fire by quick swinging motions.

The Larkin Fire Extinguisher was a bottle made of brown glass that contained a dry chemical. It had a paper label, a bottle cap style top and a mounting bracket.

When purchasing a grenade or extinguisher bottle, examine it carefully. Check for cracks, chips and repairs to the glass. Try to find examples with the original seal and contents. However, bottles without their contents are still very desirable and should be considered. Certain colors of grenades can be quite rare such as a clear Hardens or a light green Hayward.

Unusually shaped grenades are much sought after. Examples include the Kalamazoo Extinguisher which resembles a kerosene lamp chimney and Hazelton's High Pressure Chemical Fire Keg which is barrel-shaped.

Wire racks or original brackets are nice accessories to acquire. Bottle collectors as well as fire memorabilia collectors are seeking fire grenades and extinguisher bottles.

This is an open and closed view of a Shur-Stop Kit.
Set of six glass extinguisher grenades inside a red painted metal case with gold lettering on black background. These kits can still be found in older commerical buildings and were typically wall mounted.

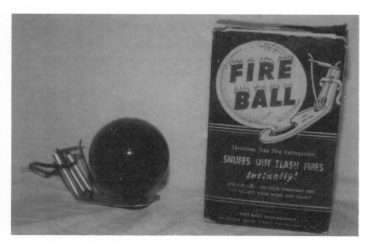

Fire Ball Christmas Tree Fire Extinguisher.

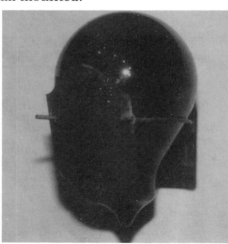

Shur-Stop Fire Extinguisher, glass bulb with red liquid contents with original bracket.

Glass Fire Grenades & Extinguisher Bottles

Display of Glass Fire Grenades.

Collection of glass fire grenades from
Central's Fire Museum, Van Wert, Ohio

3 Harden's Grenades in a Twisted Wire Basket.

Left - 2 Piece Harden's Improved Nest Grenade.
Right - 3 Piece Harden's Improved Nest Grenade
Fire Extinguisher, Rare.

1 Quart Harden's Hand Fire Grenades
in various colors.

Red Comet Fire Extinguisher,
with original label & bracket.

Glass Fire Grenades & Extinguisher Bottles

A Selection of Various Sizes, Colors and Styles of Harden's Fire Grenades.

Various Colors of Hayward's Fire Grenades.

Left: Pyrofite Fire Extinguisher Bottle. Made by Cross Mfg. Co., New York.
Center: Harden's hand grenade fire extinguisher, quilted pattern with original wire loop hanger.
Right: Marvelous fire extinguisher.

A Selection of Hayward's Hand Fire Grenades.

3 Different Colored Hayward's Grenades in a Wire Basket.

Glass Fire Grenades & Extinguisher Bottles

Autofyrstop Grenade with
bracket, 1920's.

Autofyrstop Fire Gre-
nade, small version with
bracket.

PSN Fire Grenade,
Amber.

Babcock Hand Grenade,
Non-Freezing, Amber,
Rare.

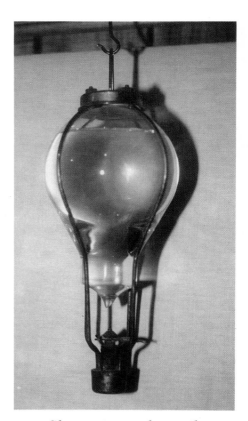

Glass extinguisher with
"Hot Air Balloon" bracket
and fusible link.

3 Different Colors of HSN Grenades
Brown, Clear & Amber.

Glass Fire Grenades & Extinguisher Bottles

Shur-Stop Fire Grenade
with bracket.

Eddison's Electric Fire Ex-
terminator, extremely rare.

Left - Flagg's Fire Extinguisher in
brown.
Right - Magic Fire Extinguisher in
amber.

Miracle fire extinguisher,
glass bulb with carbon tetrachloride. Metal holder
with fusible link. Made by
Stempel Fire Extinguisher
Co., Philadelphia.

Fire-Eye extinguisher. Red painted
glass with black embossed
bracket. Soldered bracket doubles
as a fusible link.

Hazelton's High
Pressure Chemical
Fire Keg, 1890.

Shur-Stop Fire
Extinguisher, glass
bulb with purple liquid,
red, blue and silver tag.

2 Different Versions of the Harkness
Fire Destroyer, cobalt blue.

Glass Fire Grenades & Extinguisher Bottles

Firex Fire Grenade
with fusible link
bracket.

Canteen style glass fire extinguishers.

3 Different Grenades with Railroad Markings,
used on locomotives.

Left - Kalamazoo Fire Extinguisher
in cobalt blue.
Center - Healy's Hand Fire Grenade in amber.
Right - Rockford Kalamazoo Fire Extinguisher
in cobalt blue.
Note: these grenades resemble
kerosene lamp chimneys.

Diamond Fire Grenades in olive and
brown, made by Barnum.

Glass Fire Grenades & Extinguisher Bottles

Pair of Extinguisher Bottles with fusible link hook, 1940's.

2 Different Large Grenade Extinguishers used by railroads in pullman cars.

Unusual fire eye extinguisher bottle. The purchaser of this item was told that a trucker was using this extinguisher inside the cab of his semi-truck.

Dri Gas Fire Extinguisher, Chattanooga, Tennessee.

Set of Three Glass Fire Extinguisher Bottles.
Left - Pronto
Center - Dashout
Right - Pyrofite

Glass Fire Grenades & Extinguisher Bottles

PRICE GUIDE FOR GLASS FIRE GRENADES & EXTINGUISHER BOTTLES

Fire Grenade Pricing.

1 quart Harden's, amber - $750.00
1 quart Harden's, green - $650.00
1 pint Harden's, blue, footed - $125.00
Rockford Kalamazoo - $450.00
Babcock, amber - $1250.00
Babcock, blue - $1400.00
Barnum's Diamond, olive - $550.00
Fire Ball Christmas Tree Extinguisher - $20.00
PSN, brown - $425.00
HSN, amber - $250.00
Hayward's - $275.00
Harkness Fire Destroyer, blue - $550.00
Harden's Hand Grenade Fire Extinguisher with
        original wire loop hanger - $125.00
Magic Fire - $600.00
Flagg's - $400.00
W.D. Allen - $1500.00
Little Giant - $1250.00
Red Comet Fire Extinguisher, with original label
        & bracket - $50.00
Shur-Stop - $50.00
Shur-Stop Kit. Set of six glass extinguisher grenades
        w/metal case - $150.00
Firex – $75.00
Hazelton's High Pressure Chemical Fire Keg - $300.00

Extinguisher Bottle Pricing.

Auto Fyr Stop Ext./Grenade - $60.00
Canteen style glass fire ext. - $300.00-400.00
Pyrofite - $150.00
Dri Gas, Tennessee - $200.00
Larkin - $65.00
Miracle Fire Ext., w/carbon tetrachloride
        by Stemple Fire Ext. - $65.00
C & N.W. Ry - $325.00
Shur-Stop Fire Ext., glass w/purple liq. - $75.00
Fire Eye Ext. w/fusible link - $65.00
Unusual Fire Eye Ext. bottle - $125.00
Glass Ext. w/"Hot Air Balloon" bracket - $55.00
Glass fire extinguisher with frosted bulb - $45.00
Glass grenade w/purple contents - $70.00

Wire basket, holds 3 grenades - $195.00
Wire basket, holds 2 grenades - $175.00

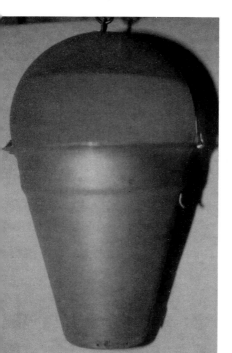

Glass fire extinguisher, frosted bulb, metal holder with internal fusible link.

Glass grenade with purple contents. Stepped, cylindrical aluminum holder, with internal fusible link. Missing hanger strap.

Auto Fyr Stop. This extinguisher could be thrown as a grenade or the top could be snapped off for use as an extinguisher bottle.

Hats & Helmets

Fire hats made their appearance around 1740. Jacobus Turck is credited with inventing these stovepipe shaped hats. In 1780, the Hand in Hand Fire Company began painting the crown of their stovepipe hats white with the initials H.H..

In 1793, a hat was made with a piece of material attached to the crown, referred to as a "frontispiece". Many scholars believe that firemen adopted the frontpiece from Hessian troops of the Revolutionary War. This may indeed be the origin of the frontpiece.

By the early 1800's, many fire companies determined that a uniform design of fire hat with lettering was necessary. This is to help identify firemen at the scene of a fire.

Many of these early fire hats were made of pressed felt, water repellent wool, paper mache, or painted oyl cloth. These hat materials were great for parades but were substandard for actual use on the fireground. Stovepipe hats were still being used as late as the 1860's.

Leather had been used all along and was more durable. Early leather helmets had no support around the brim. Heavy stitching was tried and so was wicker as a means of reinforcement. Neither method worked very well.

In 1824, Matthew DuBois added a metal wire to the brim of a fire hat. This wire eliminated the warpage the leather would undergo when exposed to heat and helped reinforce the brim.

Early leather helmets had four combs (cones). A comb is a ridge of leather where a seam is stitched together. Soon helmets were being made with eight, twelve, or sixteen combs. Presentation helmets had even more combs, 144, 180 or even 320 combs. The more combs a helmet had, the stronger it supposedly was. This wasn't always the case as some helmet makers used thinner materials and reduced the amount of leather in their higher combed helmets. Combs could be arranged in various patterns such as the basketweave.

Many fire hat manufacturers were originally harness or trunk makers and began to expand their businesses. One of the most famous and successful helmet makers was Henry T. Gratacap. In 1836 Mr. Gratacap, also a foreman in the New York Fire Department, opened up his own factory. He is most famous for developing raised hat fronts with stitched lettering. In addition, Gratacap designed the first eagle holder for the hat front. Eagle holders were made of leather during the late 1830's and early 1840's. By the late 1840's, Gratacap was making brass eagle holders. Why Gratacap chose an eagle for the holder is unclear. Some claim it was a patriotic theme due to the War of 1812. Others believe the eagle may actually be a phoenix.

Various helmet makers copied the eagle. Soon other designs of front holders appeared. Designs include a lion, tiger, seahorse, serpent, dog, fox, beaver, whippet, rooster and a fireman with a trumpet. Helmets with these types of holders are rare and are highly sought after by collectors.

Gratacap made thousands of fire helmets over a period of 32 years. The most famous and expensive helmet he made was a 180 comb, presentation helmet for a foreman of Sacramento. The helmet featured a gold and silver frontpiece with inlaid precious stones. That hat cost $1350.00 at a time when a regular helmet cost $4.00 and a presentation hat averaged about $75.00.

In 1868, Gratacap sold the business to Jasper and Henry Cairns. Cairns & Brother continued to produce the leather helmet and introduced the ventilated model. This model of helmet had tiny openings to keep the head cool. Today, Cairns is still in the business of making helmets.

Early helmets had paper labels to identify the maker. Later styles had the maker's name stamped into the brim. This practice of stamping the brim continued until about 1870. Paper labels returned for a brief period. By the turn of the century, helmets had a brass identification disc.

During the 1880's, the purchaser of a fire helmet had a huge selection to choose from. There was the jockey style, derby, South American, continental, and many other styles. Making its debut at this time was the aluminum helmet. At first, aluminum helmets were mainly owned by chiefs, since they were rather expensive. Gradually these helmets became less costly to produce. Production of the aluminum helmet continued through the 1930's. Many of these helmets had brass eagle holders and some had the other, rarer types of helmet front holders.

As the 1930's drew to a close, the fancy holders disappeared. By this time, the low front helmet was already in wide use. These helmets had a lower profile with a plain, metal front holder. One version, the "New Yorker" featured 4 combs with an inner cushioned suspension. During WW II, due to rationing, a smaller rather ugly helmet known as the "Warbaby" was used. The helmet's protective ability increased with the addition of a visor or a face shield.

Leather helmets can still be special ordered today. Most current helmets are made of lightweight, composite materials that absorb impact.

The demand, age, originality, and condition of a helmet are four important factors that determine its value. Early stovepipe fire hats are extremely rare and valuable, especially ones with elaborate illustrations or portraits. Condition is not as critical because locating one of these hats is very difficult. Leather helmets from the 1800's are excellent investments. Very rare and desirable are high front, leather helmets with unusual front holders. Watch for exposed wire around the brim, deteriorated leather, and a missing or incorrect frontpiece.

Hats & Helmets

Parade Fire Hat, pressed felt, american eagle with shield, "Perseverance" on front of hat & initialed "W.E.C." on the top of the hat, 7" tall, 1850's.

Parade Fire Hat, pressed felt,"Northern No. 1 Liberty", 6" tall, 1860's, #3 condition.

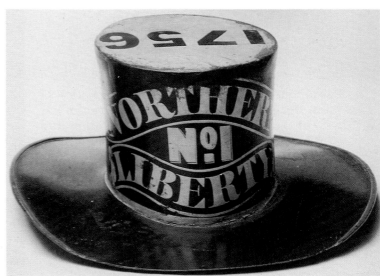

Parade Fire Hat, pressed felt, "Franklin Fire Co." with gilt shield and number "4", 5" tall, 1860's, #3 condition.

Hats & Helmets

Parade Fire Hat, pressed felt, decorated with a cen[...] medallion depicting William Rush's "Water Nymph [...] Bittern", "Fair Mount" and initialed "S.G.T.", 6" tall, 18[...] #2 condition.

Parade Fire Hat, pressed felt, with rendition of John Neagle's famous painting "Portrait of Pat Lyon at the Forge", "Mechanic Fire Comp." and initialed "J.M.W.", 7" tall, 1850, #3 condition.

Parade Fire Hat, pressed felt with portrait medallio[...] "General Lafayette", "Lafayette Hose Company" and [...] tialed "P.V.", 6 3/4" tall, 1840.

Hats & Helmets

Parade Fire Hat, pressed felt, featuring a portrait medallion of "Stephen Decatur", "Decatur F.E. Co." and marked "E.V. Bunn", 7 1/2" tall, 1850.

rade Fire Hat, pressed felt, American Eagle with land-aped background, "Columbia Hose Company" and arked with the initials "H.C.N.", 7" tall, 1850, #3 ndition.

Early Leather Wide Brimmed Helmet, 4 comb, painted red & black with gold letters, "No. 3 - E.B.D.", 5 3/4" tall, early 1800's, #3 condition.

Hats & Helmets

Felt Parade Helmet, from a German community in Philadelphia, nickel plated, spire & steamer ornament, 1860's.

Toy Texaco Fire Chief helment with microphone & speakers, 1964.

Cairns Black Leather Helmet, 8 comb, with nicely painted leather front piece.

A Pair of Jockey Style Helmets, 8 comb, worn by firemen who rode on a steamer, the short brim wouldn't bang into the apparatus.

Presentation Helmet, leather with high eagle holder. Leather front piece with 2 and 92 below. Applied silver disc with presentions on rear brim

Jockey style helment, Gratacap, embossed brass front piece with torches, axes, hoses and ladders. Applied silver #1 in center, circa 1882.

Hats & Helmets

Aluminum Helmet painted black with fire-man front holder.

Cairns Ventilated Black Leather Helmet with seahorse holder.

Early pressed felt helmet, seamless crown with "KEYSTONE" and #1 in gold, circa 1840.

Fox front piece holder.

L.E. Olson & Sons Leather Helmet, 8 comb, with lion front holder.

Seahorse front piece holder.

Hats & Helmets

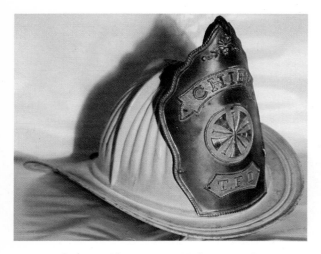

Cairns Aluminum Helmet with brass front piece.

Cairns Leather Helmet, 8 comb, from a Hook & Ladder Co.

High eagle helmet, leather, 64 comb made by Anderson & Jones. Front piece is nickel over brass with applied numbers 14 and 1869.

Leather helmet with lion front piece holder. Nickel-plated front piece with applied brass letters. VIGILANT #1 S.F.E. Co.

Cairns Aluminum Helmet with high eagle front holder, 1900.

High eagle helmet, aluminum with metal front piece, Captain 1 P.F.D.

Hats & Helmets

Cairns Black Leather Helmet, 8 comb, with leather eagle front holder.

Leather Helmet, 16 comb, low front design, painted white, 1940's.

Leather helmet, 4 combs with flat brim. Faded white leather front piece with gold lettering "WASHINGTON #2".

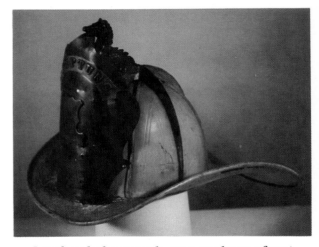

Leather helmet with rare seahorse front piece holder. Painted white with gold accents. Brass front piece with worn silver plating and missing letters. "NEPTUNE 1".

Cairns Black Leather Helmet, 8 comb, with high eagle front holder.

Low front white leather helmet, with hand painted front piece "Deputy Chief S.F.F.D".

Hats & Helmets

Fiberglass Composite Helmet with faceshield, 1950's.

Display of Leather Helmet Fronts.

MSA Skull Guard, "1 - M.F.D.", 1940's.

Cairns & Bros. Helmet, model #900, late 1950's, early 1960's.

Helmet with faceshield, Federal Signal Corp., Model FH2 - Series A3.

Derby-style helmet, black leather with white leather front piece. "FIRE POLICE" 1 W.F. paper label on inside reads "Smith Mfg. Co." - Circa 1880.

Hats & Helmets

Cairns Leather Helmet, 4 comb, with whippet frontpiece holder.

South American Style Leather Helmet w/eagle frontpiece holder.

Leather "New Yorker" Helmet, 4 comb.

Leather "War Baby" Helmet, WW II era.

Leather Helmet w/torch.

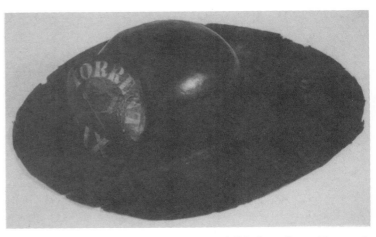

Torch boy's helmet. Early pressed felt hat from Torrent Six. Roxbury on rear of brim, circa 1790.

Hats & Helmets

Also pictured on page 114

Left - Leather Jockey Style Helmet w/gold braided chin strap
& stamped brass front shield w/silver #1.
Right - Black Leather Jockey Style Helmet w/silver F.D.
buttons.

Stove Pipe Parade Hat, pressed felt.

Early Style Leather Helmet, 4 comb,
w/handpainted frontpiece, 1850.
Also pictured on page 117

Leather Jockey Style Helmet
w/rare fox frontpiece holder.

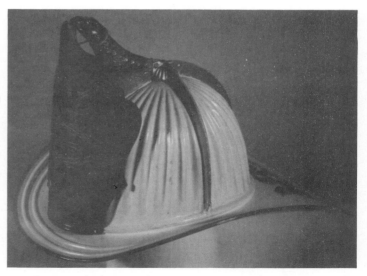

High eagle helmet, aluminum with brass front piece
with intertwined letters "HECO".

Hats & Helmets

No. 171.—LEATHER BADGES. The above badges are designed for either the helmet or fatigue caps. Made of black leather.

Lettered, with panel for firemen's caps, per doz.	The above of red, white or blue **patent**
" in panel, half lined and stitched "	leather, extra....................
" in panel, full lined and stitched "	

No. 172.—HELMET CAP. Made of black enameled leather, with best leather peaks, with seams corded with leather; a very nice, light, durable hat, without badges.......................
Red, white or blue patent leather, without badges.. ....
Red, white. blue, or black enameled cloth, with imitation leather peaks, without badge......
For price of badges, see illustration and description of No. 171.

No. 173.—FATIGUE CAPS. Best cloth caps, leather peaks, silk lined...........
Best flannel caps, leather peaks, well lined ....
Gold gilt or silver gilt wreaths, with number of company, same as shown on cap No. 174, are 25c additional.
Campaign Caps, the above shape or military shape, made of enameled cloth, any color suitable for parades not lined, and made cheap................................

No. 174.—N. Y. REGULATION. This style, made of the best blue cloth, lined throughout with leather and hair cloth, with spring top, so as to retain shape, trimmed with Fire Department buttons. This is the finest cap that can be made ....
The same shape, of red, white or blue enameled leather..........................
Wreaths in gold or silver gilt, as shown in the illustration, are 25 cents a cap additional. For price of leather lettered badges for the above, see No. 171.
Gilt embroidered wreaths, with name for officers, etc ... .

Hats & Helmets

SIXTEEN CONE FIRE HAT.

FIG. 92.

The Sixteen Cone Hat, with plain front and rim
With Extra Fancy Stitched Front, One Dollar Extra.
By dozen, with plain rim and front

IN ORDERING HATS, SEND SIZE OF HAT WORN.

EIGHT CONE REGULATION.

FIG. 93.

The above cut represents the Regulation Fire Hat adopted and approved by the department generally, and has been in popular use a number of years. These goods are made of the best oak-tanned leather thoroughly seasoned and hardened and warranted for service. We have made improvements in the manufacture of this hat which enables us to produce a light weight, yet strong and durable article.
Price, in Black, per doz.

LIGHT SERVICE HAT.

FIG 94.

Light Service Hat, similar to the Eight cone, with the exception that it has eight small cones and no high ones, the Frontispiece being smaller and the entire hat much lighter. This is a cheap hat for Parades and Light Duty, being very neat.
Price, in Black Lustre, per doz.

Helmet Cap (High Cone) with Eagle Tip.

A very showy hat for parades.   Thousands now in use.

Patented April 11, 1876.

Helmet Cap No. 4.

Entered according to Act of Congress by Fred. J. Miller in the year 1876.
Helmet Cap No. 4 of "Alaska" leather, * with Eagle, Tiger or Beaver and Maple Leaf Tip and new style front.

Eight-Cone Centennial Hat.

The Centennial Hat is made of stiff, hard leather—same as the old-fashioned Fire Hat.
4 cone,   black,   8 cone,   black,
1 "   white or red.   8 "   white or red.

Continental Cap.

Entered according to Act of Congress by Fred. J. Miller in the year 1876.
Continental Cap, made of enameled cloth of any color, with lettered front, per doz.
Continental Cap, made of "Alaska" leather*
* The "Alaska" leather has proved after fifteen years' hard service in a large number of fire departments in the United States, Canada and South America, to be the best material from which to make Fire Caps. It is soft, pliable, waterproof, will not fade, *and will not crack from extreme heat or cold.* When parties wish caps made of the smooth enameled leather, we will furnish them at same price as given for "Alaska" leather.

THE DERBY HAT.

FIG. 95.

The new improved Derby Hat is made of regular Fire Hat Leather, thereby making a durable, light and handsome hat ; just the thing for parade and light service.
Price, Black, per doz
If Red, White, or any other color

EIGHT CONE HELMET.--No. 1

FIG. 96.

Per dozen, black   Any other color

HIGH CONE HELMET.

FIG. 97.

The eight cone No. 2 and eight cone Helmet are made of the same material as the Regulation Hat.
Price, Black, per doz.   Any other color

FIREMEN'S HATS, SHIRTS, &c.

Our facilities for the manufacture of personal equipments, of best material, finish, and latest styles are unsurpassed by any house in the country. Samples and estimates for outfits for Departments, Companies or individuals, cheerfully furnished on application.

The New Improved Corrugated 64 Cone Fire Hat.

FIG. 90.

This addition to our List of Hats are principally for parade or light duty. The Hat is light and very fancy ; it is the handsomest Regulation Hat made and becomes more popular every season. According to our new Improved Machinery we can offer them for nearly the same price as the Old Style Regulation Hat.
Price, Black   per doz.   Price in Colors

Our Thirty-two Cone Hand-Sewed Hat.

FIG. 91.

For Department and Company Officers, Presentations, Prizes, Fairs, etc., with embossed Brims and Ventilating Cones and Linings made up in the best possible manner. These hats are very popular and desirable for presentation to newly elected company officers and department commanders. We make them of a superior quality of best oak-tanned leather and finished with nickel or gold-plated crest, silk linings, embossed brims and painted fronts, etc., and can be made light, medium or heavy weight, as desired.

PRICE LIST, PER HAT, WITH PAINTED FRONT AND EMBOSSED BRIM.

8 Cone		48 Cone		96 Cone	
12 "		56 "		104 "	
16 "		64 "		120 "	
24 "		72 "		136 "	
32 "		80 "		148 "	
40 "		88 "		164 "	

Hats & Helmets

FIRE HATS.

Seventy-two comb hat, fancy rim. These hats are especially suitable for presentations and tournaments. Prices vary according to style of front and amount of fancy work on rim.

32-COMB HAT.

With patent ventilating combs and linings.
Price, in Black, ...
" other colors, ...

This addition to our list of hats is designed principally for parade. The hat is not only light, but also a very close imitation of our fine fancy hats which, by reason of their cost, have been practically beyond the reach of companies. The combs are embossed, and their number (32) selected with reference to appearance on parade. They are about ⅜ of an inch apart, and show to much better advantage than if the number were greater. It is decidedly the handsomest regulation hat we make, and is becoming more popular every season.

This is the regulation 8-comb hat for paid and volunteer departments, and is made of best oak-tanned hard leather.
Black, with colored front, per

FIRE HATS.

Eight-comb Helmet, is made of same material as regulation hat, No. 130.
Price, in Black, ...
" Red, White or other colors, . . .

68-COMB HAT.

With patent ventilating combs and linings.
Price, in Black, ...
" other colors, ...

A HANDSOME AND UNIQUE DESIGN.

In this hat an entirely new feature is introduced, namely: that of curving and intersecting the small combs, thereby producing the handsome effect as shown in the cut. The design adds not only beauty but strength, as the intersecting combs constitute a series of cross-bracings calculated to give stiffness to the skull of the hat.

8-COMB HELMET.

With patent ventilation.

Other Black Colors.

Price, Stitched, 8-comb, per doz., .
Price, Embossed, 32-comb, per doz., .
Price, Embossed, 68-comb, per doz., .

METALIC CORRUGATED FIRE HAT.—Something New.

Combining strength, durability and lightness. The most economical and serviceable fire hat ever worn by a fireman. It always keeps in form. Price same as leather hats.

METAL FRONTS FOR HATS.

Metal fronts are becoming quite popular for strictly parade dress. They make a very showy appearance and add greatly to the attractiveness of the uniform. We have numerous designs appropriate to the different branches of the service. Price ranges from $2.50 to $4.00 each, according to ornamentation. Estimates furnished separately or in connection with hats or helmets.

A   B

NEW STYLE CAP DEVICES.

Nickel or Gilt, with centre designs, reverse color.

D   C

No. C.—Price, as shown in cut, .
    " with H. & L. emblem, .
    " with name of Company engraved in plate in centre, .
No. D.—Price, with figure, . .
    " with H. & L. emblem, .

REGULATION CAPS.

With improved Spring Crown and Hair-Cloth Support. Warranted to hold its shape and give satisfaction.
Price, in our A quality Blue Cloth, Indigo Dyed, per doz., .
Price, in our B quality Blue Cloth, Indigo Dyed, per doz., .

ENAMELED LEATHER FATIGUE CAP.

Price, Black, per doz. with Front, .
    " in Colors " " .

WHITE DUCK CAPS.

With double cover and skeleton frame, so that one cover can be in the wash while the other is in use
Best Linen Duck with two Covers, per doz., .
    " " " one .
    " Cotton " " extra Cover, .
    " " " " " one .

Hats & Helmets

SERVICE HELMETS
ALUMINUM

The Cairns One-Piece Aluminum Helmet has been standard in many departments for thirty years. It is growing in popularity, each year adding many more users. Its combination of light weight, strength, graceful lines and good wearing qualities make it a very desirable headgear.

NO SEAMS TO LEAK

CAN'T SHRINK

LIGHT : STRONG

DURABLE

CAIRNS No. 350 ONE PIECE
Aluminum Helmet

This Helmet is made of the best rolled aluminum. The crown and brim are drawn up from one piece. There are no seams nor riveted joints The hat will not leak and it cannot shrink. The crown is corrugated for greater strength and is given additional protection by four heavy combs. It is finished in the best of enamels in standard colors: black, red, or white; special colors to order. The Helmet is regularly fitted with a lining which conforms to the shape of the head, distributing the weight over the entire crown of the head and thus adding comfort. This lining is easily removable for cleaning, airing or renewal, a sanitary feature which is of real value.

Black Helmets—With lettered fronts and regular felt lining ....
With cushion lining (see pg. 4) ....
Ear Laps (see pg. 6) Add ....
Red or white helmets, add ....

Helmet Hanger for suspending helmets from rail of apparatus. Snaps into ring on helmet brim.

A substantial strap and buckle with harness snap. Keeps helmets out of the way of hose and other equipment. yet always in readiness.

No. 390

NEVER GO TO A FIRE WITHOUT THE PROTECTION OF A GOOD HELMET

No. 5A LEATHER SERVICE HELMET WITH No. 240 FRONT FOR CHIEFS AND ASSISTANT CHIEFS

Any Leather or Aluminum Helmet can be furnished as here pictured.

No. 240 Front

5 Trumpets for Chief
3   "   " Asst. Chief
2   "   " 2d Asst. Chief

No. 240

SERVICE HELMETS
MODIFIED STYLES

The regulation helmet is occasionally modified to meet special conditions. A few of these modifications have been quite widely adopted and we are prepared to supply them when so ordered.

We are always glad to exchange views with department chiefs and to supply special features if practical to do so.

No. 359
SCROLL HEAD AND MEDIUM HEIGHT FRONT

No. 360
PLAIN HEAD AND LOW FRONT

There is a tendency to reduce the height of the helmet by using lower ornaments and fronts. The regular eagle head stands about 8" high, the scroll No. 359 about 7" and the plain holder No. 360 about 5½".

The lower styles shown above—while not as ornamental nor as heroic in appearance as the Eagle Head—have advantages from the standpoint of utility. They balance better on the head and are not so apt to be knocked off when working in close quarters. All grades of Cairns Helmets—Leather and Aluminum may be trimmed as above shown. Prices, same as regular helmets.

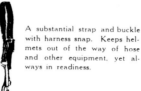

For those who prefer a smaller brim we can furnish a style as shown opposite and known as the Derby. Any of our leather or aluminum helmets may have this style brim. The Derbies may be had with eagle head or with the special heads shown in figs. 359 and 360.

No. 352 DERBY

FRONTS FOR HELMETS

Front Plates for the Helmets are an important feature, as they serve not alone to improve the appearance of the helmet, but also as identification of the organization, its branches, and its officers. We can furnish a great variety of designs but show only a few as these will give a general idea of what is used. Our leather fronts are made of the best patent leather, neatly cut and stitched. The lettering is set in panels, which are artistically arranged and a combination of colors used to make the name stand out clearly. See color plate, page 25.

No. 220   No. 230   No. 240   No. 365

SPECIAL FRONTS FOR OFFICERS
(See color illustration page 24)

Styles No. 220 and No. 230 are hand painted fronts, ground work in pure gold leaf, designs and lettering in oil colors artistically applied. Styles 240 and 365 are white patent leather with lettering in raised leather letters on contrasting colored panels. Insignia in gold leaf. They are neatly stitched and formed.

	Separate Fronts	If with complete helmet add to price of helmet
Prices: Nos. 220 and 230 ea.		
Nos. 240, see page 24		
No. 365		

Officers helmets are furnished with regular lettered fronts as shown in figures 361 and 20 without extra charge. They are white patent leather with raised leather letters and sunk panels in contrasting colors. They may have other lettering to suit with company numbers, etc.

PRICE

Each, if furnished separately

No. 361   No. 20

Cairns Fronts Are Reinforced With a Metal Brace Which Holds Them in Shape

Hats & Helmets

PRESENTATION HELMETS

Among Volunteers and Regulars alike it has become the custom when making presentations to their officers to choose articles which have a service as well as a sentimental value. There is nothing more appropriate than the helmet, and this is often supplemented by the white or black rubber coat, rubber boots, etc. For Captains (Foremen), and Lieutenants (Asst. Foremen) it is customary to use the regular 8 Comb service helmet with an inscribed plate on the brim. For Chiefs and Assistant Chiefs the regular 8 Comb pattern as illustrated on page 24 is often used. The special designs as illustrated and described below are also popular.

No. 10
64 Comb Helmet, Hand Made

The illustration shows a hand-made helmet in the 64 Comb pattern. This is made up of the best of grain leather selected for light weight. It is neatly shaped, all Combs are stitched, the design on the brim is embossed and stitched, it is lined with soft moleskin and satin and the finish is in the best of enamels. It is a superior article in every way and makes a desirable gift. Made in three patterns, 32, 48, and 64 Comb at following prices.

No. 10 Hand-made Helmet with all gilt hand-painted front No. 220   32   48   64
and with Engraved gold-plated presentation plate to fit over Comb Comb Comb
embossed shield on brim

No. 8A
32 Comb

We can also furnish the No. 4, No. 8, or No. 6 styles with the Combs embossed. Embossed design on brim and with soft moleskin and satin lining like illustration No. 8A. Price if with No. 220 front $12.75, if with No. 240 front $10.75. Extra for gilt inscription plate $2.50 to $3.00.

In the paid departments the choice for presentation is usually the Regulation Reinforced Helmet as described on page 5, also see color plate page 24. It may be had in 8, 12, or 16 Comb pattern built for service with cushion lining and ear laps at the following prices:

	8 Comb	12 Comb	16 Comb
White Helmets and No. 220 front			
White Helmets and No. 240 front, see page 24			
White Helmets and regular front			

SERVICE HELMETS
LEATHER

THE TOUGHEST
LEATHER HELMET
EVER MADE

Noted for its
DURABILITY
COMFORTABLE FIT
GRACEFUL APPEARANCE

CAIRNS No. 5A CITY SERVICE
Heavy Leather Helmet—Reinforced

"Regulation" Wherever Leather Helmets Are Used

This hat is made from the best quality of grain leather specially tanned to give toughness and selected for uniform thickness. The completed hat is put through a special process which hardens the leather so that it will hold shape and resist heat. The best of materials, careful workmanship and a final finish of specially prepared paints, combine to produce an article of great durability and pleasing appearance.

Reinforcement—To prevent shrinkage and warping out of shape, a fault of all ordinary leather hats, the Cairns Patented Flanged Reinforcement was devised. This consists of a metal band secured to the base of the skull inside of the lining and made with a flange extending over the edge of the brim. This flanging of the metal makes it rigid and positively prevents shrinkage. The Cairns Reinforced Hat will stand up under severe service and will hold its size and shape in a manner unknown to any other leather hat. Note the metal plates at the base of the combs. These plates straddle the comb and are riveted through into the flanged metal reinforcing band, binding the brim, the crown and band securely together.

Comfort—A lining which conforms to the shape of the head distributes the weight of the hat over the entire crown of the head thus adding greatly to the comfort of the wearer and also affording unusual protection against shock from falling objects.

Chiefs of Departments are demanding the best in head-gear for their men, and the Cairns No. 5A Heavy Leather Service Hat—Reinforced, meets the demand. This hat is standard throughout this and other countries, in fact wherever leather hats are used. It will outwear any other hat made.

Finished in standard colors—black, red, and white. Other colors to order.

Black Helmets—with lettered fronts and regular felt lining
With cushion lining (see pg. 4)
Ear Laps—(see pg. 6) Add
Red or white helmets, add

NEVER GO TO A FIRE WITHOUT THE PROTECTION OF A GOOD HELMET

PARADE HELMETS

The three styles illustrated below are primarily intended for parade use. They may be made up with different style heads and fronts but are usually made as shown in the regulation pattern. They all present a very pleasing appearance and like all Cairns Leather Helmets are made of the best of grain leather and are of first quality in material, workmanship, and finish. They are lower in price than the service helmets because of lighter weight and not because of inferior quality.

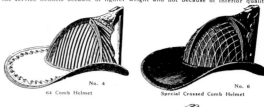

No. 4
64 Comb Helmet

No. 6
Special Crossed Comb Helmet

No. 8
32 Ccmb Helmet

Prices—including lettered front pieces on any of above styles,

No. 379

Unless otherwise ordered helmets are made with the Eagle Front Holder. We can supply when wanted, however, the Fireman or Tiger Holder as illustrated, or with special holders as shown on page 8.

No. 380

Black   Colors

No. 22

Prices given above are for helmets with regular leather fronts. See pages 12 and 13. For parade use, the fancy metal front is often used. See No. 22. Usually made in polished nickel with embossed design in gilt. Can be had in various designs, the prices varying with style and quantity ordered. Prices on application.

HELMET CAPS
Made of "ALASKA" ENAMELED CLOTH.

No. 6

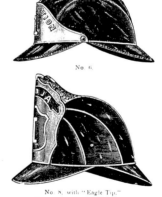

No. 8, with "Eagle Tip."

No. 8, with "Beaver and Maple Leaf" Tip.
Price. No. 6 complete, with lettering on front,
" No. 8 "eagle," "tiger," or "beaver and maple leaf" tip and high front,
SAMPLES SENT TO ANY PART OF THE COUNTRY FOR EXAMINATION.

MILLER'S 64-CONE CORRUGATED FIRE HAT,

The Lightest, Strongest, Handsomest and Most Comfortable Hat yet Invented.

Made from Hard, Stiff Leather, same as the old style Fire Hat, and supplied with a perfect ventilator.

MILLER'S "64 CONE CORRUGATED" FIRE HAT.

(First Brought Out January 1879.)

"The regular Eight Cone Stiff Leather Hat was originally adopted by the fire departments of New York, Boston and New Orleans about the year 1821, as the most suitable hat for service and parade, for the reason that it was stiff and would resist a blow from falling slates or bricks; the brim carrying off the water and preventing the water from running down the neck of the wearer, or when the firemen were compelled to fight the fire a close that the heat would be unconfortable for the face, the hat could be reversed on the head, bringing the wide por of the br m in fr nt to protect the face from being burned. Immediately after the introduction of the Eight-Cone Hat, in the cities mentioned above it was adopted by all the fire departments then in existence as the regulation hat. This hat supplied all that was desired for the firemen's use, and the more it was used for service and parade the more it became established as "just the thing."

In the cut- are shown the latest improvements in the manufacture of Stiff Cone Leather Hats, of the Regulation style-the invention of Fred. J. Miller, of this city (who by the way has originated nearly all the new styles of firemen's uniforms introduced for many years past,) which he has named the 64-cone Corrugated Hat, for the reason that it has 64 cones instead of eight-the Cones being made by machinery, instead of sewed as formerly. By the improved process of manufacture he is enabled to produce a thoroughly practical Hat—one that is stiffer, stronger and lighter than any yet offered to the fire man, besides being the handsomest and most comfortable."

64-CONE CORRUGATED FIRE HAT.

WITH "EAGLE," "TIGER" OR "BEAVER AND MAPLE LEAF" TIP AND NEW STYLE FRONT.

Price of Black Hat. | Price of Red, White or Blue Hat.
With Plain Front.

OLD STYLE 8-CONE FIRE HAT.

Made of Hard, Stiff Leather, with "Eagle," "Tiger" or "Beaver and Maple Leaf" Tip.
With new style of front, lettered with na or and No. of Company, and with white metal wreath, with raised representations of the different apparatus used in the fire department. Sample of this new style of front sent to any address for approval.

4 cone, black, ... | 8 cone, black, ...
4 cone, white, red or blue .... | 5 cone white, red or blue,......

Helmet Caps.

Helmet Cap No. 1.

Price of "Alaska" leather, * plain front, per doz. . . . . .
" " " fancy " " . . . . .

Helmet Cap No. 2.

Entered according to Act of Congress by Fred. J. Miller, in the year 1876.
Price of "Alaska" leather, * of any color, plain front, per doz .
" " " " " " fancy front, "

Helmet Cap (with high cone) No. 3. *patented April 11, 1876.*

Price of "Alaska" leather, * of any color, plain front, per doz.
" " " " " " fancy front, "

*The "Alaska" Leather has proved after nearly fifteen years' hard service in a number of the Fire Departments of the United States, Canada and South America, to be the best material from which to make Fire Caps. It is soft, pliable, waterproof, and will not crack from extreme heat or cold. When parties wish caps made of the smooth enameled leather we will furnish them at same price as given for "Alaska Leather."

Fatigue Caps.

CLOTH FATIGUE CAP WITH WREATH AND NUMBER.

Cloth Cap of best material, any color,
with fancy lettered front. ....
Same style, plain front. ....
" "Alaska" Leather, any color "
fancy front. ....
Enameled Cloth Fatigue Cap any
color, plain front .... "

Cloth Cap of any color, with new style
plated or gilt wreath and number in
front, of best material. ....
Same style, second quality material "
Glazed Covers, cotton........... . "
" " silk .... "

CLOTH FATIGUE CAP WITH LEATHER FRONT.

SPECIAL HELMETS

If quantities are sufficient we are prepared to design and manufacture helmets of special styles and shapes for fire, military and industrial purposes. Correspondence solicited.

No. 30 | No. 32

No. 30 and 32 illustrate two patterns of the Roman Type Helmet which are widely used in South and Central American departments. These helmets may have different styles of ornamental front holder if desired.

Per dozen
Black | Colors

Prices—No. 30 8 Comb. Light Weight for Parade
Medium Weight for Service
No. 32 Embossed Light Weight
Medium Weight
Leather Chin Straps, extra

Hats & Helmets

Parade hat, stovepipe with hand painted lettering & illustration, early 1800's - $4500.00-8500.00+
Early 4 comb leather fire helmet with hand painted frontpiece, 1850's - $2250.00
Jockey style leather helmet with fox frontpiece holder & hand painted leather frontpiece - $1500.00
Cairns 8 comb leather helmet with early style leather eagle frontpiece holder - $950.00
Cairns 8 comb leather helmet with brass eagle frontpiece holder - $950.00
Cairns aluminum helmet with eagle frontpiece holder & brass frontpiece - $650.00
L.E. Olson & Sons, 8 comb leather helmet with lion front holder - $800.00
Cairns ventilated black leather helmet with seahorse frontpiece holder - $950.00
16 comb leather helmet, low front design, painted white, 1940's - $175.00
Cairns 8 comb black leather helmet with nicely painted frontpiece
        "Chief Engineer" & brass eagle holder - $750.00
Aluminum helmet, painted black with fireman front holder & leather frontpiece - $800.00
Modern, composite helmet - $50.00-100.00
Felt parade helmet, nickel plated spire & steamer ornament, from a German
        community in Phil., 1860's - $350.00
Parade hat, "Engine 2" black with gold trim - $3000.00
Parade fire hat Columbia Hose Company, pressed felt with hand painted American Eagle
        with landscaped background, 1850, 7" tall, initialed H.C.N. - $15,000.00
Parade fire hat, "Lafayette Hose Company" pressed felt with hand painted portrait of
        General Lafayette, 1840, 6 3/4" tall initialed P.V. - $9000.00
Parade fire hat pressed felt American Eagle with shield, "Perseverance",
        initialed W.E.C., 7" tall, 1850's - $1500.00
Parade fire hat pressed felt with portrait medallion of Stephen Decatur,
        Decatur F.E. Company, E.V. Bynn, 7 1/2" tall, 1850 - $25,000.00
Parade fire hat pressed felt with rendition of John Neagle's painting "Portrait of Pat Lyon at the Forge"
        Mechanic Fire Company, initialed J.M.W., 7" tall, #3 condition, 1850 - $14,000.00
Parade fire hat pressed felt decorated with a central medallion depicting William Rush's
        "Water Nymph and Bitern" Fairmount initialed S.G.T., 6" tall, 1854 - $11,000.00
Parade fire hat pressed felt "Franklin Fire Company", gilt shield with numeral "4", 5" tall,
        1860's, #3 condition - $700.00
Early leather wide brimmed helmet, 4 comb, painted red & black with gold letters
        "No. 3 E.B.D.", 5 3/4" tall, early 1800's, #3 condition - $4000.00
Jockey style helmet, black leather with silver "F.D." buttons, frontshield has "CC" - $750.00-1,000.00
Jockey style leather helmet, gold braided chin strap & stamped brass front badge
        with silver #1 - $850.00-1100.00
South American style leather helmet with eagle frontpiece holder - $1000.00
4 comb leather "New Yorker" helmet - $250.00-325.00
"War Baby" helmet, leather, WWII era - $195.00
MSA Skull Guard, "1-M.F.D.", 1940's - $45.00-65.00
Cairns & Bros., model #900, late 1950's early 1960's - $100.00
Helmet with faceshield by Federal Signal Corp., model FH2-series A3 - $75.00
Toy Texaco fire chief helmet with microphone and speaker, 1964 - $65.00
Jockey style helmet, Gratacap, circa 1882 - $1500.00
Early Pressed Felt Helmet, circa 1840 - $3500.00
High Eagle Helmet, 64 comb made by Anderson & Jones, with applied numbers 14 and 1869 - $1500.00
Leather helmet with lion front piece holder, lettered "Vigilant #1 S.F.E." - $1500.00
Leather Helmet with 4 combs and flat brim, lettered "Washington #2" - $3000.00
Presentation helmet, leather with high eagle holder - $1500.00
Leather helmet with rare seahorse front piece holder, lettered "Neptune 1" - $1750.00
Derby-style helmet, lettered "Fire Police", and paper label reads "Smith Mfg. Co." circa 1880 - $1750.00
Torch boy's helmet, from Torrent Six, Roxbury on rear of brim, circa 1790 - $4500.00
High eagle helmet, lettered "HECO" - $1250.00
High eagle helmet, lettered "Captain 1 P.F.D." - $1250.00
Low front white leather helmet, lettered "Deputy Cheif S.F.F.D." - $450.00

Hose

The use of hose to carry water can be traced back to 400 B.C., when Athenian firemen filled ox gut casings with water. As the casings were squeezed or stepped upon, water would squirt out and could be used to extinguish fires.

It wasn't until 1672 that the first practical fire hose was invented by Jan and Nicholaas Van de Heijden. Made of leather which was stitched together, this early hose leaked and would not withstand much pressure.

To improve this condition, Sellers and Penock devised a riveted leather fire hose in 1807. The rivets were made of copper and were used to bind the seams. It was said that a hundred feet of hose was the equivalent of sixty men with buckets.

Unfortunately, leather hose was heavy, weighing approximately 85 pounds per 50 feet of length with couplings. Leather hose was also prone to cracking and rotting. A better hose was needed.

Rubber hose was the answer. In 1821, James Boyd received a patent for a rubber lined, cotton webbed fire hose. Rubber hose was first used in 1871 by the Cincinnati Fire Department. Since then, rubber hose has been produced with synthetic fabric reinforcement layers. Hose comes in sizes ranging from 3/4" to 6" inside diameters.

The most desirable hose to collect are lengths or segments of leather fire hose. It is sometimes difficult to find sections in decent condition. Many restorers of early hose wagons and apparatus are seeking this type of hose.

Later style, rubber lined, cloth hose can be an inexpensive way to enhance a display of fire collectibles.

Riveted leather fire hose, 50' length.

Collection of various sizes of smooth bore nozzles used on hand lines.

WOODHOUSE LEATHER FIRE HOSE.

THE STANDARD

TRADE MARK.

OAK LEATHER HOSE.

FIG. 112.

There being some departments that still adhere to the use of the time-honored Leather Hose we are prepared to furnish the best grade of Oak-Tanned Double or single riveted. There is no better.

PRICES.

2 inch . . . .
2½ inch . . . .

HOSE JACKETS.

Neeley's Hose Leak Stop.

Meets a want long felt for a means of stopping leaks or bursts in hose. Is lined with rubber, and provided with racks on the outside, which so securely bind the hose that the water cannot escape. Can be applied or removed instantly.

Price . . . .

FIG. 66.

Open.

Closed.

FIG. 67.

Heavy Leather, per dozen $18 00

HOSE AND LADDER STRAPS.

FIG. 68.

FIG. 69.

Nothing more materially lessens the labor of the fireman than the use of a strap, not only in carrying the hose from one point to another, but in carrying it up a ladder; the hoseman can rest at intervals by placing the hook over any of the rounds of the ladder. One very important thing is the freedom of action it gives the pipeman in directing the stream to much better advantage, as he is relieved of the weight of the hose, no matter at what point on the ladder he may be engaged. They are quickly adjusted, and a glance at the above figure will show how easily it can be done. All the fittings are made of galvanized iron.

Price . . . .

Hose

HOSE SUSPENDERS.

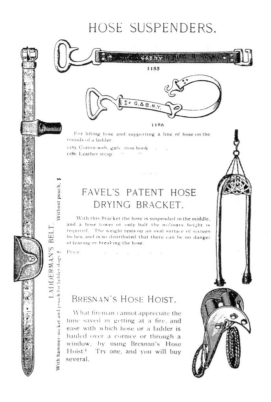

1185

1186

For lifting hose and supporting a line of hose on the rounds of a ladder.

1185 Cotton web, galv. iron hook
1186 Leather strap

(vertical text at left) LADDERMAN'S BELT. Without pouch, $ With hammer socket and pouch for ladder dogs, $

FAVEL'S PATENT HOSE DRYING BRACKET.

With this Bracket the hose is suspended in the middle, and a hose tower of only half the ordinary height is required. The weight rests on an oval surface of sixteen inches, and is so distributed that there can be no danger of tearing or breaking the hose.

Price.

BRESNAN'S HOSE HOIST.

What fireman cannot appreciate the time saved in getting at a fire, and ease with which hose or a ladder is hauled over a cornice or through a window, by using Bresnan's Hose Hoist? Try one, and you will buy several.

Miller's Hose Jacket, or Repaier.

The damage to property by water, caused by the bursting of hose, especially when a hose is laid through a building, is obviated by placing of a perfect length of hose that will not burst under the pressure. A Hose Jacket or Repairer is made, the engineer using it as a receptacle for it. If Fire Companies have it and ready for action, it saves the loss of their engines or hose carriages when required to save the flow of water. The great saving of loss is so complete every year will see the importance of every fire company in the country supplying themselves with this Hose Jacket.

THE EXCELSIOR WAREHOUSE HOSE REEL.
STATIONARY

PATENT SWINGING HOSE RACKS.
Japanned Red.

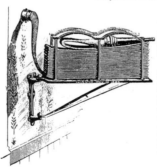

FIG. 131

We make the above in Brass, if desired, and submit prices on application.

Nos. 5 and 6 will carry heavy hose of almost any make in 50 feet lengths.

We can supply any of the following sizes bronzed in gold at same figures, if so desired, or Nos. 0, 00, 1, 2, 3, and 4 nickel plated or brass, finished to order, at an additional cost of $3.00 each, net.

FOR UNLINED LINEN HOSE.

No.	Size of Hose.	Full capacity
0.	for 1½ or 2 inch	50 feet
00.	" 2 "	50 "
1.	" 1½ or 2 "	100 "
2.	" 2½ "	100 "
3.	" 1½ or 2 "	150 "
4.	" 2½ "	150 "

For Rubber-Lined Linen or "Mill" Hose.

No.	Size of Hose.	Full capacity
3.	for 1½ or 2 inch	50 feet
4.	" 2 "	50 "
6.	" 2 "	100 "

UNIVERSAL HOSE REEL.

This Hose Reel is designed for fastening to barn, tree or any convenient place. Hose can be unreeled in any direction. Its capacity is about 150 feet 1-inch garden hose. Being made of wrough iron it is made strong and durable.

Hose

18" Length of Riveted Leather Hose.

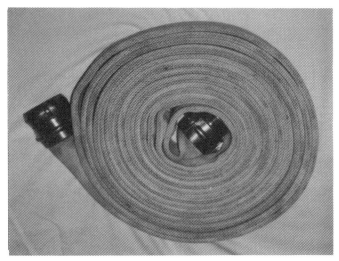

50' Roll of Rubber Lined Cloth Hose,
2 1/2" with brass couplings.

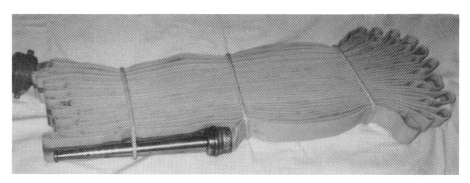

50' Bundle of Cloth 1 1/2" Hose with brass nozzle.

PRICE GUIDE FOR HOSE

12" length of leather hose - $85.00
50' length of riveted leather hose, rare - $1500.00
50' length of 1 1/2" rubber lined hose - $30.00
50' length of 2 1/2" rubber lined hose - $35.00
50' length of 3" rubber lined hose - $40.00
50' length of 4" rubber lined hose - $45.00
50' length of 5" rubber lined hose - $60.00

Hydrants

In the early 1800's, municipal waterworks used gravity fed reservoirs to supply an underground system of hollowed cypress logs. In order to obtain water, firemen dug down to a log, bored a hole, and filled their engines from the bubbling opening in the log. When water was no longer needed, the hole was filled with a wood plug. This is how the word "fire plug" originated. Often times, rival fire companies would fight over access to the water. This necessitated the practice of a fire company to enlist a prizefighter to guard the water supply. These men were called "plug uglies". Sections of old wooden water mains are collectible, and have value as educational and display items.

The first fire hydrant was invented by Frederick Graff of Philadelphia in 1801. This hydrant was T-shaped and had a fire hose connection on one side and a drinking spigot on the other side. The first hydrants were made by an ironworks that casted cannon barrels for the revolutionary war. It is interesting to note that the main body of a fire hydrant is known as the barrel.

Since those early days many different manufacturers of fire hydrants appeared. Some hydrants were very large with multiple outlets, others were rather small with only one or two outlets. Hydrants usually were made with cast iron barrels and had brass threaded outlets and operating nuts.

Most desirable for a fire collectible display are very small hydrants with ornate designs cast into the barrel, or miniature hydrants with working parts that were salesmen's samples. These hydrants were popular after the turn of the 20th century. Avoid buying a very heavy hydrant with part of the main attached. Usually, a great amount of grief is required to transport one of these hydrants. Don't be too discouraged if you find a nice old hydrant with several layers of cracked paint. Take the hydrant to a commercial paint stripper. The stripping is inexpensive and the clean metal of the hydrant will be ready for repainting.

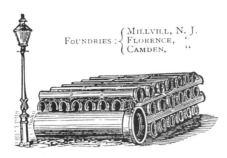

FOUNDRIES : { MILLVILL, N. J.
FLORENCE, "
CAMDEN, "

OFFICE:
400 CHESTNUT STREET,
PHILADELPHIA, PA.

R. D WOOD & CO.,

MANUFACTURERS OF

CAST IRON PIPE

FOR WATER AND GAS,

Mathews' Patent Fire Hydrants,

SINGLE AND DOUBLE-VALVE.

EDDY VALVES,   LAMP POSTS,

JONVAL TURBINES,   HEAVY MACHINERY,

GENERAL CASTINGS,   FLANGE PIPE.

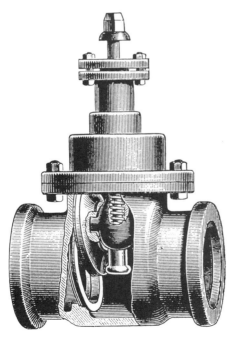

Hydrants

Early Cast Iron
Fire Hydrant.

Ornate Fire Hydrant
with 2 outlets.

Chromium Plated Fire Hydrant.

Fire Hydrant.

Hydrants

American Darling Fire Hydrant.

Kennedy Fire Hydrant.

Eddy Fire Hydrant.

Wood Water Main Section, 10" diameter, 2" thick, made of cypress.

Hydrants

PRICE GUIDE FOR HYDRANTS

Small, pre-1900 hydrant with 2 1/2" outlets and cast design in the barrel. - $350.00
Chrome fire hydrant - $375.00
Modern, standard style hydrant - $200.00
Wood water main section, 7" diameter, 3" long, made of cypress - $125.00
Salesmen's sample hydrant with working parts - $500.00-650.00

Door Guards

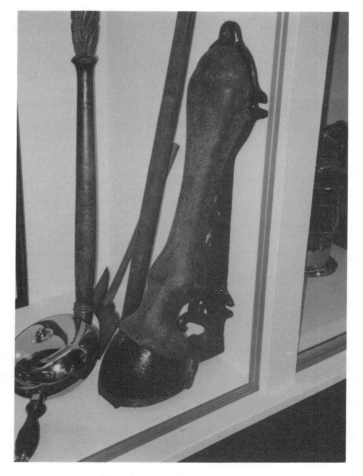

Fire house door guards.
Used to prevent wheels on horse drawn aparatus
from catching on main doors, circa 1850.
$450.00 per pair

Ladders

Ladders were used as early as 1200 A. D. by the cliff dwellers of New Mexico. In colonial times a ladder was often mounted to the outside of a building along with several fire buckets. In this manner the ladder was handy in case of a fire. Ladders have always been and still are, essential pieces of equipment that a fire department uses.

The basic types of ladders most departments employ is the straight ladder, extension ladder, roof ladder, attic ladder and the pompier ladder. Straight ladders and extension ladders can be used to access an upper level of a building for search and rescue or fire extinguishment. Roof ladders have hooks that hold onto a roof peak. Attic ladders allow access to openings where space is at a minimum. Pompier ladders have a gooseneck hook that allows firemen to climb to points beyond the reach of other ladders. Many years ago most ladders were made of wood. Modern ladders are constructed of aluminum and fiberglass.

Small, old wood ladders used by fire departments make nice display items. Look for wood ladders used on early motorized fire engines. These ladders are generally smaller and when mounted on a wall can really enhance a display of fire collectibles.

Ladders and Extension Ladders.

"WIRE-STRENGTHENED" SAFETY LADDER.

WIRE-STRENGTHENED LADDER.

This is the strongest and lightest ladder in use. By the addition of the wire rope, which runs entirely around the side rails of the ladder, and which adds but little extra weight, it will support more than double the weight.

PRICES.

10 to 20 feet, one coat paint
20 to 30   "   "   "
32 to 45   "   "   "

EXTENSION LADDER.

(STILLMAN'S PATENT—NOT ON WHEELS.)

From 40 to 75 feet,
        Ironed and Painted.

EXTENSION OR SPLICE LADDER.

(MILLER'S PATENT.)

For Villiage Trucks, 20 and 18 foot to be used together or separate ; can be used of any length from 20 to 32 feet. Price, complete, ironed and painted one coat lead color.

COMMON LADDERS.

(MADE TO FIT ANY TRUCK)

10 to 20 feet, ironed and one coat of paint,
22 to 30   "   "   "   "
32 to 45   "   "   "   "

BANGOR EXTENSION LADDER.

No. 1, 24 feet, extends to 40 feet....
 "   2, 29   "   "   50 " ....
 "   3, 34   "   "   60 " ....
 "   4, 37   "   "   65 " ....

Ladders

Wood Ladder, 10' when fully extended.

PRICE GUIDE FOR LADDERS

Wood straight ladder, 10' in length - $85.00
Roof ladder, wood w/steel hooks, 8' in length - $125.00
Extension ladder, wood, 2-piece, 15' fully extended - $150.00
Pompier ladder - $175.00-200.00

Lanterns

There are several types of fire department lanterns. One type is known as the working lantern. Working lanterns were carried on fire apparatus and were removable for use at the fire scene. These lanterns had a cage with a water shield to protect the lamp chimney, and a wire loop hanger. Two popular working lanterns were the Dietz Fire King and Fire Queen lanterns. The Fire King was made from 1907-1940 and was available in several finishes. These included polished brass, nickel plated brass, bright tin, bright tin with copper front and silver-plated brass.

The Fire Queen lantern was produced from 1901-1910 and came in polished brass or nickel-plate. Globes for these lanterns were available in clear, red, green, blue or a two color combination of glass. Bulls eye lenses of different colors could be fastened to the globe plate to identify an officer's lantern.

Some examples of lanterns are stamped with the names of fire apparatus manufacturers, such as Seagrave, American LaFrance or White, making these lanterns very valuable. The Eclipse was another famous lantern. This lantern was touted as the finest one ever made. Eclipse lanterns are rare and highly collectible.

Another type of lantern was the Chief's lantern. Lanterns of this variety were generally smaller than working lanterns. Chief's lanterns had a large bail handle that could be used to carry the lantern on the arm. Brass or nickel plating was the standard finish. Glass globes could be ordered in a variety of colors, with or without engravings.

Wrist lanterns were similar to Chief's lanterns, except they featured a small carrying ring instead of a large bail handle.

The most desirable lanterns are presentation lanterns. These lanterns were presented as gifts of honor to firemen. Presentation lanterns featured engraved globes and were often silver plated. An example in fine condition with the original globe would command a high price. Lanterns that were converted into table lamps often have holes drilled in them, which greatly reduces their value.

Dietz Fire King lantern with embossed "White" on wind-break. Nickel-planted steel with clear globe.

Fire King with mounting bracket used to secure lantern on apparatus.

Wrist lantern. Polished brass with etched cobalt blue globe.

Lanterns

FIRE DEPARTMENT LANTERNS.

FIG. 62.

The Eclipse Lantern is the only lantern that will not go out by smoke, having air chambers which allow perfect safety to firemen entering smoky buildings.

FIG. 63.

Tin,
Brass,

PATENT REFLECTING HAND LANTERNS.

They throw a very powerful and brilliant light for fully one hundred feet ahead.

Japanned,
Brass or Oriode,
Nickle or Silver, Full Plated,

FIG. 63.

FIRE DEPARTMENT LANTERNS.

All Brass, with Wire Guard and Wind Shield.

PRICES.

All Brass, Polished,
       Nickeled.

THE ECLIPSE LANTERN.

PATENTED SEPT. 5, 1888.

THE BEST LANTERN MADE FOR FIRE DEPARTMENTS AND GENERAL USE.

Cannot be Blown Out!
Will not Jar Out when Carried on Apparatus!
Smoke does not affect it!

PRICES

All Brass, Polished,
    " Nickel Plated.

LANTERNS.

PATENT REFLECTING LANTERN.

Will throw a powerful light fully one hundred and fifty feet ahead of lantern, and will give more light than three ordinary lanterns. They have locomotive reflectors and improved burner, and will burn perfectly kerosene or mineral or sperm oil without a chimney.

Size of Glass, 3½ inches, brass............................
    "   "   3½,   oriode............................
    "   "   3½,   nickel............................
    "   "   3½,   silver............................
Colored and engraved glass, in back............................

SQUARE LIFT TUBULAR.

F. D. TUBULAR LANTERN.

Heavy Copper Bottom.

Per dozen............................
Nickel-plated, per dozen............................

Lantern Holders for Apparatus.

Plate 191.

This is the strongest and best holder made. Has strong double spring, which prevents lanterns getting loose by any possibility.

PRICES.

Iron, japanned......
Polished brass.......
Nickel Plated brass...

——————

In ordering lantern holders specify for what make of lantern.

Plate 190.

Plate 191.

Lanterns

Lanterns.

Patent Reflecting Lanterns.

Will throw a powerful light fully one hundred feet ahead of lantern, and give as much light as three common lanterns. The best lantern for Chief Engineers now made.

Japanned, ...
Brass, ...
Nickel, ...

If with glass behind reflector, and lettered, $2 each additional.

Improved Fire Department Lantern.

No. 5.—Lantern can be lighted and the wick regulated from the outside without removing the globe or oil cup. Globe can be taken out, which is a great convenience in cleaning.

Brass, *white glass* . . .
Nickel, " . . . .

Engraving on globe, 75 cents extra.

FIRE DEPARTMENT LANTERNS.

11 inch high.
FIG. 61.

HAND LANTERN No. 1, N. Y. F. D., TUBULAR, FOR KEROSENE.

Tin, ; nickel plated,
Tin, with copper bottom, ; nickel plated,

No. 1 TUBULAR LANTERN.

With Patent Tube Extinguisher.

Burner is No. 1 5-8 Inch Wick

FOR KEROSENE.—Can be regulated, filled, lighted and extinguished without removing the globe.

No. 1 Tubular Lanterns, no Guards,
" 1 " with
" 0 " no "
" 0 " with

FIG. 65.

Chief's lantern, brass with green and clear globe.

Chief's Lantern.

Plate 184.

Small and handsomely finished with large bail handle to carry on the arm.

Colored globes may be fitted at extra cost. See page 93.

Plate 183.

No.
3. Polished brass . . . . .
3. Brass, nickel plated "
39. Brass, not shown . . . "
39. Brass, nickel plated "

Plate 184. No. 3.

"Square Lift" Fire Department Lantern.

(TUBULAR.)

Plate 182.

Polished brass . . . .
Brass, nickel plated . . . . .

Mill Lanterns.

Similar in construction to Plate 182; heavy tin. Can be locked, when lighted, so that workmen cannot raise globe.

With padlock . . . .
Without padlock . . . .

Fancy Lanterns.

Plate 183.

For parade and ornamental display. Hexagonal with colored glasses. Front glass engraved with name or number of company, and other glasses with attractive designs. All metal parts nickel plated.
Price . . . .

Plate 182.

Lanterns

Six Sided Presentation
Lantern, made by
Gleason & Bailey.

Early Tole Wristlet
Candle Lantern.

Dietz Fire King Lantern,
nickel plated, clear globe.

Dietz Fire King Lantern,
polished brass,
with ruby globe.

Lanterns

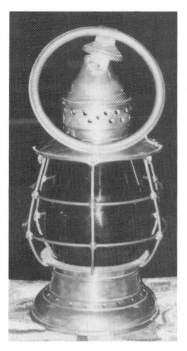

Brass Wrist Lantern
with ruby globe.

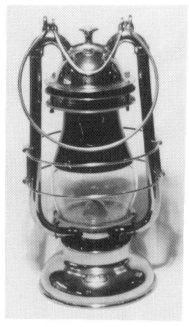

Eclipse Presentation Lantern, nickel plated.

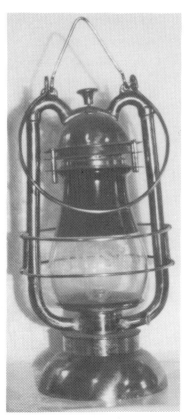

Eclipse Lantern, nickel plated with replacement globe.

Brass Wrist Lantern, red & clear glass with "Chief Engineer" etched in globe, made by William Porter & Sons, New York, 1880's.

Lanterns

Chief's Lantern, polished brass, clear globe, by Peter Gray of Boston.

Wrist Lantern, nickel plated, used on a steam fire engine, made by W. Porter & Sons, 1880's.

Brass Chief's Lantern, note the large bail handle.

Pair of Dietz Coldblast Lanterns, circa 1920.

Left – Ham Lantern, nickel plated, clear globe, 1905.

Right – Dietz Fire Queen Lantern, nickel plated, clear globe, 1905.

Lanterns

Price Guide for Lanterns

Eclipse lantern - $1250.00
Dewey lantern, painted steel with two color globe - $400.00
Dietz Fire King, brass with red globe - $375.00
Dietz Fire King, steel, painted red with brass reservoir - $275.00
Dietz Fire King, nickel plated, marked "Seagrave" - $650.00
Dietz Fire King, nickel plated, marked "White" - $1000.00
Dietz Fire King lantern with embossed "White" on windbreak. Nickel-plated steel with clear globe - $1000.0
Dietz Fire Queen - $550.00
Red globe for Dietz lantern - $35.00
Chief's lantern, brass with red globe - $500.00
Chief's lanter, brass with green and clear globe - $950.00
C.T. Hamm, coldblast lantern, brass with clear globe - $350.00
Wrist lantern, brass, with fire dept. markings, made by Wm. Porter & Sons - $450.00
Wrist lantern, marked "Learys" about 1870 - $450.00
Wrist lantern, polished brass, with etched cobalt blue globe - $500.00
Presentation lantern, Dietz Fire King, silver plated with engraving - $1000.00-1500.00
Tole lantern with brass finial, clear globe with etched "2" and bail handle - $350.00
Early tole wristlet lantern, painted "7" on glass panel - $650.00
Six sided presentation lantern made by Gleason & Bailey, etched sea shells &
        plant designs, "Rhinebeck, Hose #1" - $7,000.00
Presentation chief's lantern, nickel plated brass, red & clear globe - $1500.00-2000.00
Presentation lantern, nickel-plated. Etched name and floral designs on blue and clear globe - $1750.00
Fire King lantern with mounting bracket used to secure lantern on apparatus - $425.00

Presentation lantern,
nickel-plated. Etched
name and floral designs
on blue and clear globe.

Dewey Lantern.
Painted steel with
two color globe.

Wrist type lantern
"Learys" about
1870, brass with
clear globe.

Liquor Decanters

Liquor decanters are decorative bottles or vessels used for serving alcoholic beverages. Over the years, several distilleries have produced liquor decanters in a variety of firemanic themes. These decanters can be found in the shapes of firemen, dalmatians, nozzles, hydrants, fire engines and the maltese cross.

Collectible liquor decanters are more valuable when full, with an unbroken seal. However, many collectors and dealers sell only empty liquor decanters to avoid any legal liabilities.

Early Lionstone decanters have become quite valuable. Jim Beam produced some nice decanters featuring fire apparatus. Many collectors buy what appeals to them personally.

Band Box/Hat Box

Band box or hat box showing a fire company
with hand drawn apparatus going to a house fire.
$250

Liquor Decanters

Jim Beam Liquor Decanter,
1928 Fire Chief's Car.

Liquor Decanter,
1927 Ahrens Fox.

Jim Beam Old Mississippi Steamer
Liquor Decanter.

Liquor Decanters

Fireman with
Hose, made by
Lionstone Liqueur
and bottled by
Lionstone Distill-
eries Ltd., Bard-
stown, KY.

Fireman with Axe,
Old Commonwealth
Kentucky Straight
Bourbon Whiskey,
bottled by J.P.
VanWinkle & Son.

Fireman Holding
Child, made by
Lionstone Liqueur,
bottled by Lionstone
Distilleries Ltd.,
Bardstown, KY.
1974 Fireman #2
with child.

Harmony Liquor Decanter,
Old Commonwealth Kentucky
Straight Bourbon Whiskey,
bottled by J.P. VanWinkle &
Son.

Fireman Taking Pulse & Giving
Oxygen Liquor Decanter, Old Commonwealth Kentucky Straight Bourbon Whiskey, bottled by J.P.
VanWinkle & Son.

Liquor Decanters

PRICE GUIDE FOR LIQUOR DECANTERS

(EMPTY).

Jim Beam, 1934 Fire Chief's Car - $85.00
Jim Beam, Old Mississippi Steamer - $100.00
Ezra Brooks, Antique Fire Engine Steamer, 1971 - $75.00
Ezra Brooks, Firefighter, 1975, fireman with axe - $45.00
Sky Country, 1923 Ahrens-Fox, VFD #7 - $175.00
Old Mr. Boston, Mooseheart F.D. - $85.00
Old Commonwealth, fireman with axe - $75.00
Old Commonwealth, "Harmony" - $75.00
Old Commonwealth, fireman taking pulse and giving oxygen - $75.00
Lionstone, #1, fireman, 1972 - $275.00
Lionstone, #7, fireman with hose - $175.00
Lionstone, #2, fireman holding child - $175.00
Lionstone, #3, fireman sliding down pole with dalmation - $75.00
Wild Turkey, 75th Anniversary of Mack Trucks, 1975 - $75.00
Mount Hope Estate & Winery, Going to the Fire, 1983 - $85.00

FRAMED CERTIFICATES

Membership certificate by Currier & Ives
with original gilt composition frame, dated 1891.

Fireman's Honorable Discharge
Certificate date 1862 with gilt composition frame. *Note:* Certificate has
water stains and foxing. Frame features helmet, trumpets, axes, pike
poles, ladder, torches, hydrants, hose
& nozzles. Restored.

Models & Kits

Models of fire apparatus are miniature examples of the real thing. Often times a fire laddie would craft a model of his company's apparatus. Apparatus builders had intricate, working salesmen's samples made to scale. On occasion, a beautifully detailed model was presented as a gift.

Examples of models include hand tubs, hose wagons, hose carriages, steamers, hook & ladders and motorized fire engines. Models can be constructed of wood, metal, plastic or a combination of materials. Some models were built with moving parts, working pumps and can actually squirt water.

Model kits were designed to be assembled by a fairly skilled individual as a project. Unopened model kits with the plastic wrap still intact are more valuable than assembled versions.

Generally, the finer the detailing and quality of craftsmanship, the greater is the value of the model. Models built during the 1800's are very desirable. Try to find a complete model. In some cases it is possible to fabricate parts for incomplete models.

Models & Kits

Model of a 1911 Christie Steam Fire Engine.

Hand Made Model of a Parade Hose Reel, 1835.

Models & Kits

Working Model of a Hand Engine "14", A.C. McKinley, maker, New York, 19th century, painted scene on pump chamber depicts a fireman beside a monument with a fire beyond; model includes suction hoses, mounted brass plate inscribed "A.C. McKinley Maker New York", lg. 39, wd. 13 1/2". Note: A.C. McKinley was the father of President McKinley.

ass and Wood Working Model of a Steam Fire gine, America, 19th century, boiler mounted h brass plate inscribed "Hope", lg. 48, wd.

Plastic Model Kit of the Backdraft Pumper by Monogram.

Models & Kits

PRICE GUIDE FOR MODELS & KITS

Model Pricing.
Hand pumper, wood & metal, finely detailed, early 1800's - $3500.00-10,000.00
Handmade model of a parade hose reel, 1835 - $4500.00
Hose carriage, wood & metal, built to scale - $2500.00-5000.00
Brass and wood working model of a steam fire engine, American made, boiler with brass plate
     inscribed "Hope", 48" long, 17" wide - $35,000.00
Steam fire engine model, wood & metal, hand built - $2500.00-7500.00
Working model of a hand engine "14", made by A.C. McKinley, New York, painted scene on pump
     chamber depicts fireman beside a monument with fire in the background, 39" long,
     13-1/2" wide - $25,000.00

Model Kit Pricing.
Revell, chemical & ladder, 1953 - $45.00
Revell, fireboat NYFD - $55.00
Revell, water tower, 1950's - $65.00
Lindberg, American LaFrance Pumper - $45.00
AMT Fire Chief's car, Chevrolet - $50.00
AMT rescue van, Chevrolet - $50.00
Monogram, "Backdraft" pumper - $15.00

Muffin Bells

Muffin bells were warning devices that became popular in the 1800's. Similar to rattles in that both devices served the same purpose, the muffin bell was a later innovation. A town watchman, upon discovering a fire would ring the muffin bell. A muffin bell is constructed of two round shaped bell halves. Each half of the bell halves is a clapper. When the bell is swung back and forth it makes a "cling-clang" sound. The bell halves are attached to a turned wood handle. On the handle is a lanyard ring for carrying the muffin bell. Sizes of these bells range from 3" to 7" in diameter. As a general rule, the larger the muffin bell, the more valuable.

Polished brass muffin bells with turned hardwood handles;
sizes 5³/₈", 5³/₄". 6" & 7".

Muffin Bells

6" Muffin Bell, brass with turned
wood handle.

PRICE GUIDE FOR MUFFIN BELLS

3 1/2" muffin bell with wood handle - $300.00
4" muffin bell with wood handle - $325.00
4 1/2" muffin bell with wood handle - $350.00
5" muffin bell with wood handle - $400.00
5 3/8" muffin bell with wood handle - $450.00-650.00
5 1/2" muffin bell with wood handle - $450.00
5 3/4" muffin bell with wood handle - $450.00-650.00
6" muffin bell with wood handle - $550.00
7" Muffin Bell with wood handle - $650.00 (Rare)

Mugs

There are two basic categories of fire collectible mugs, occupational shaving mugs and beverage mugs. Occupational shaving mugs became popular after the Civil War and could be found in barbershops across the country. A fireman would purchase a shaving mug with his name or initials and leave it at the barbershop. When the fireman returned for a shave, the barber would use the fireman's own personalized shaving mug. These mugs were usually decorated with colorful designs of helmets, steamers or fire scenes. Most mugs had lettering and accents done in gold. Occupational shaving mugs are generally older and more valuable than beverage mugs. Some shaving mugs are reproductions and are difficult to tell from originals because of their fine quality.

Beverage mugs are the other category of fire collectible mugs. Hundreds of different styles of mugs have been produced over the years. Mugs were given away or sold at musters, exhibitions, conventions, parades and other fire related events. Some mugs are shaped like boots. Others resemble nozzles or steins. Most mugs have firemanic designs and usually have the date of the event on the mug. Beverage mugs are fairly common and relatively inexpensive.

Mugs

Moustache Cup – modern,
by Knobler of Japan.

Reproduction Shaving Mug
by Viking.

Left - Occupational Shaving Mug, colorful horse drawn
steamer with gold lettering.
Right - Reproduction Mug given out by Warner Lambert
in the early 1950's.

Mugs

PRICE GUIDE FOR MUGS

Occupational shaving mug with picture of horse drawn apparatus, gold accents &
   owner's initials - $550.00-850.00

Reproduction shaving mug, Fireman by Viking - $25.00

Reproduction shaving mug given out by Warner Lambert, 1950's - $85.00

Beverage mug, standard type - $10.00-15.00

Beverage mug, unusual shape - $35.00-45.00

Royal Doulton, Toby Jug Fireman - $125.00

Music, Sheet

Many popular ballads of the 1800's had a fire fighting theme. Firemen were considered heroes by the community and scores of songs were dedicated to firemen or fire companies. Composers would write polkas, quick steps, marches and waltzes for hook & ladder companies, hose companies and individual officers or firemen.

Often, the covers of sheet music were lavishly illustrated with color lithographs or engravings. Some fire companies such as Forest Engine Co. #3 of New York, had a singer present during large fires. In this manner the firemen could listen to music while working the hand operated fire engine.

The lyrics of many songs were entertaining and often touted a fire company's skill. For example, this is an excerpt from the "Providence Fireman" dated 1886:

Peal out ye fire bells in a dreaded tone,

The firemen will protect the property we own.

Let the fiery flames leap high in the air,

The Providence Firemen will do and dare.

When buying sheet music examine it carefully. Check to make sure there are no missing pages. Watch for rips, torn corners, stains or yellowing of the paper. All of these conditions detract from the value of the music. Be especially careful of sheet music that has been trimmed. On occasion, sheet music was trimmed smaller to fit in a folio or music book. The trimming process can sometimes remove a printed dedication that greatly reduces the value of the sheet music.

Early sheet music from the 1840's - 1860's is particularly desirable. In addition, music with colorful lithographs of apparatus or fire scenes are highly collectible.

Music, Sheet

The Fire Signal March by
George W. Moraine, 1912.

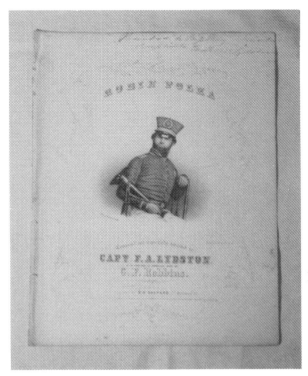

Robin Polka by G.F. Robbins, composed &
respectfully dedicated to the Captain of the
Ocean Hose Co., 1853.

On Fire by Edger Leslie.

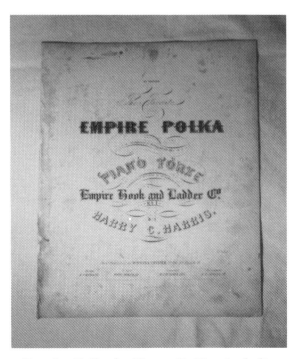

Empire Polka by Harry C. Harris dedicated to Empire Hook & Ladder Co.
No. #1, 1852.

Music, Sheet

Hylas Quick Step dedicated to Captain A.C. Goodman of the Hartford Sack & Bucket Co., 1850.

Fire & Flame by Marie Louka, very colorful illustration.

To The Rescue by Harry J. Lincoln, 1920.

The Fire at the Hotel Windsor by R.H. Brennen & Pauline Story.

Music, Sheet

Our Brave Heroes by Eugene Mack.

The Firemen's Song by Maurice E. Swerdlow, 1919.

False Alarm by Harry J. Lincoln.

Only a Man by Charles I. Ryan, 1901, hand colored print.

Music, Sheet

Homeless Tonight or Boston in Ashes by
L.A. White, beautifully colored lithograph of
two young girls fleeing the great Boston fire.

PRICE GUIDE FOR SHEET MUSIC

Jerry Moran, The Fearless Fireman, by Henry Traxles and Eddie Nelson, 1911 - $40.00
The Fire Bell Galop, 1855 - $75.00
Fire Drill, by Harry J. Lincoln, 1909 - $45.00
Hylas Quick Step, dedicated to Capt. A.C. Goodman of the Hartford Sack & Bucket Co., 1850 - $225.00
The Fire Master, by Harry J. Lincoln, 1904 - $80.00
To The Rescue March, by Harry J. Lincoln, 1920 - $40.00
Fire Alarm March, by Harry J. Lincoln, 1905 - $40.00
Fire & Flame, Marie Louka - $75.00
The Fire at the Hotel Windsor, R.H. Brennen/P. Story - $35.00
On Fire, Edger Leslie - $45.00
Empire Polka, Harry C. Harris, dedicated to the members of Empire Hook & Ladder, 1852 - $75.00
Robin Polka, G.F. Robbins, composed & respectfully dedicated to the Captain of the Ocean
        Hose Co. of Springfield, Mass., 1853 - $100.00
Only A Man, Charles I. Ryan, 1901 - $100.00
The Fire Signal March, George Morraine, 1912 - $45.00
The Fireman's Song, Maurice E. Swerdlow, 1919 - $35.00
False Alarm, Harry J. Lincoln - $40.00
Our Brave Heroes, Eugene Mack - $50.00
Homeless Tonight or Boston in Ashes, L.A.White - $100.00

Nozzles and Playpipes

In 1725 the first continuous stream pumper, the Newsham, was patented. This hand operated pumper had a gooseneck nozzle mounted on top. Nozzles evolved from stationary mount to being attached to the ends of hoses.

It wasn't until 1888 that John R. Freeman experimented with several shapes and sizes of nozzles. He was successful in finding a design of a nozzle that would produce the best fire stream.

Since then, hundreds of different styles of nozzles have been produced. Some nozzles are solid stream nozzles, and may or may not have a shut-off valve. Other nozzles are adjustable from a fog to a straight stream. Smaller, solid stream nozzles are fairly common. Expect to pay more for nozzles with shut off valves as they were more expensive to produce.

Some nozzles were designed to attach to the end of a playpipe. Early playpipes were made of leather and had leather handles. Some brass playpipes had a leather covering or were wound with cord. This acted as insulation, when a fireman had to hold the cold playpipe and nozzle for a long period of time. Early nozzles with leather playpipes and handles are the most valuable, as are large nozzles and playpipes with engraving.

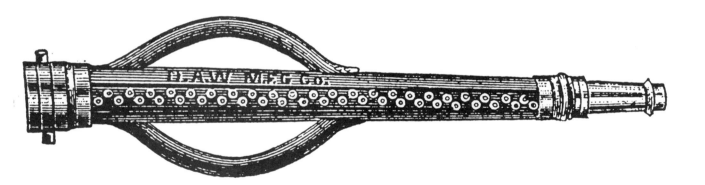

COMBINATION
CONTROLLING NOZZLE!

FIG. 32.

This valuable product, resulting from the application of much study and experience with different kinds of nozzles, and with recent improvements in its make-up, stands to-day, after over ten years practical service, the best yet produced.

While practical experience has proven the fact that at most small fires more damage is caused by water than fire, the wisdom of using a good controlling nozzle is unquestioned, and

NO FIRE DEPARTMENT CAN AFFORD TO DO WITHOUT THEM.

This Nozzle is made upon honor of the best material for service, and its durability can be guaranteed. The combinations are such that they can be changed instantly from a full stream of ¾ to 1¼ inches, to a stream and spray, or a complete spray as shown in the above cuts. For recommendations I refer to those in use.

Both in Freezing Cold, and Warm Climates.

Spray and Solid Stream Nozzle.

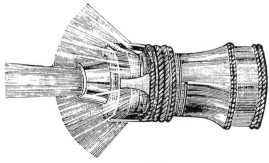

FIG. 33.

The above cut shows solid stream and spray combined; can be closed to solid stream. It is frequently the case that, if the fireman could reach the seat of fire without much delay, it might be easily extinguished, but by reason of the dense smoke he is held in check until the fire gets under good headway, and often beyond his control. And we do not hesitate to say that from repeated trials the spray nozzle has proven itself to be one of the most effective weapons in the hands of the fireman for fighting smoky fires ever brought into service, as by means of the spray the smoke is driven from in front of the fireman, and he can advance without fear of suffocation, as the spray keeps a cool current of air in front of him, he having at the same time the full efficiency of the solid stream. By simply turning the cage that holds the nipple, the spray is shut off, thereby securing a clean cut, solid stream.

Nozzles and Playpipes

BRESNAN'S PATENT HOSE-HOIST and DISTRIBUTING and CONTROLLING NOZZLES.

The above cut shows the Bresnan Hose Hoist in operation in three different positions. The action of the distributing nozzle when used at a roof fire and for basement and sub-cellar fires is very clearly shown by the illustration. It also shows the distributor connected with stationary pipes in basement, with connection with hose from apparatus or hydrant outside

Distributing and Controlling Nozzle.

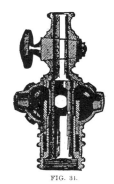

By which firemen can extinguish fires in cellars, on roofs, and between decks of ships, where pipemen cannot penetrate at the early part of the fire. Then by the Controlling Nozzle finish up the fire.

Fig. 34.—Distributing and Controlling Nozzle.

Fig. 35.—Distributing Nozzle, to be attached to hose or stationary pipes in Warehouses, Stages of Theatres, or Covered Docks.

FIG. 34.

FIG. 35.

See cut, opposite, of Distributer, at work on roof and in cellar attached to hose.

Nozzles and Playpipes

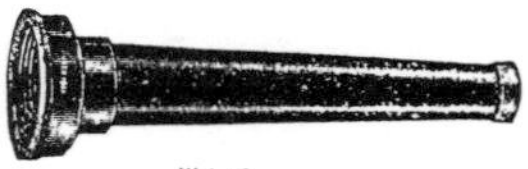

FIG. 25.

SHORT CAST HOSE PIPES—Plain.

Size	3-4	1	1 1-4	1 1-2	2	2 1-4	2 1-2
Length, inches	8	9	10	10 1-2	11	12	20

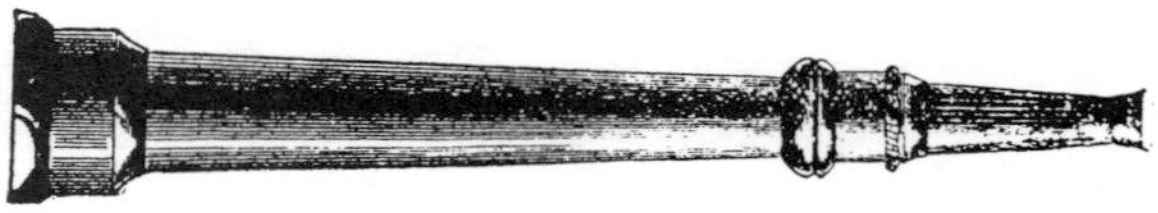

FIG. 26.

SHORT CAST HOSE PIPES—Screw Tip.

Size	3-4	1	1 3-4	1 1-2	2
Length, inches	8	10	11	12	15

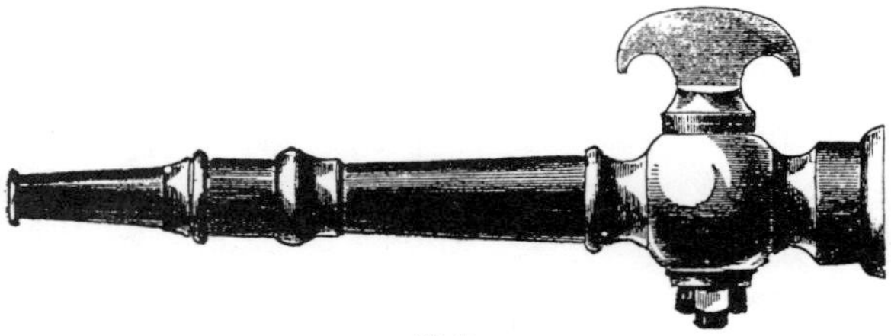

FIG. 27.

SHORT CAST HOSE PIPES—Cock on Large End.

Size	3-4	1	1 1-4	1 1-2
Length, inches	8	10	11	12

SPRINKLERS.

1 1-2 in. for 3-4 and 1 in. Hose Pipes, per dozen……
2 " " " " " ……
2 1-2 " " " " " ……

HOSE PIPES.

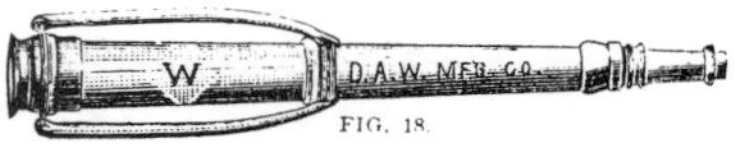

FIG. 18.

2 inch, Rubber Play Pipe, Leather Handles……
2½ " " " " ……

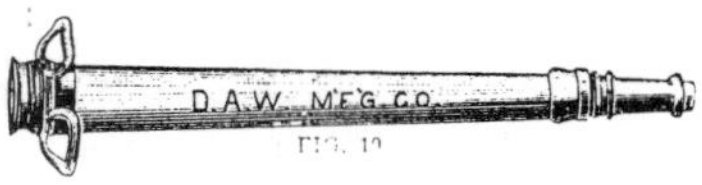

FIG. 19.

2 inch, Rubber Play Pipe, Metal Handles……
2½ " " " " ……

(Plain Butt Pipes Deduct $1.00)

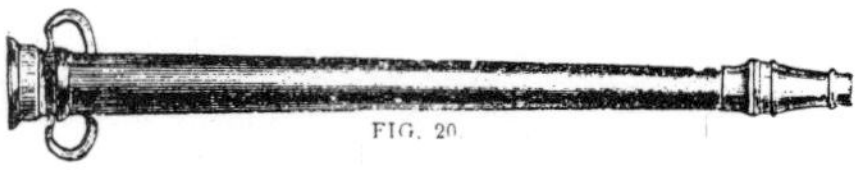

FIG. 20.

BRASS PLAY PIPES.

2, 2¼, 2½ inch, 30 inch, Screw Nozzle, Metal Handle……
2, 2¼, 2½ " 36 " " " ……
2, 2¼, 2½ " 30 " Fixed Nozzle, " ……
2, 2¼, 2½ " 36 " " " ……

(Winding and Painted, $1.00 extra net.)

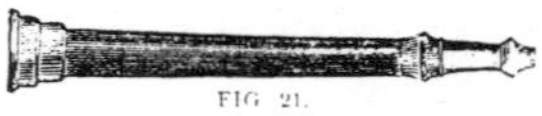

FIG. 21.

1½x15 inch, Plain Butt, Screw Nozzle……
2, 2¼, 2½x20 " " " ……
2, 2¼, 2½x30 " " " ……
2, 2¼, 2½x36 " " " ……
2, 2¼, 2½x20 " Fixed Nozzle……
2, 2¼, 2½x30 " " " ……
2, 2¼, 2½x36 " " " ……

HOSE PIPES.

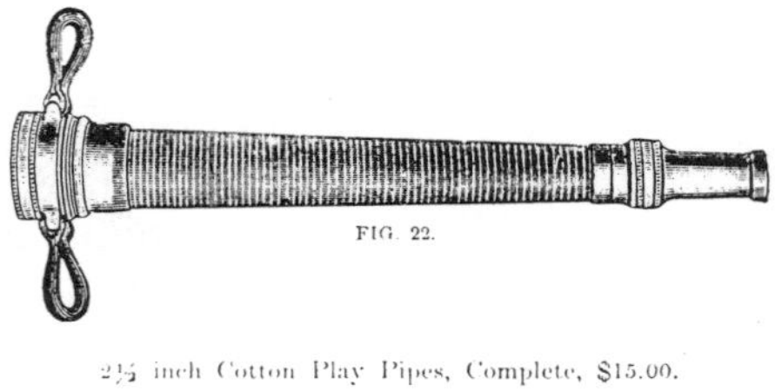

FIG. 22.

2½ inch Cotton Play Pipes, Complete, $15.00.

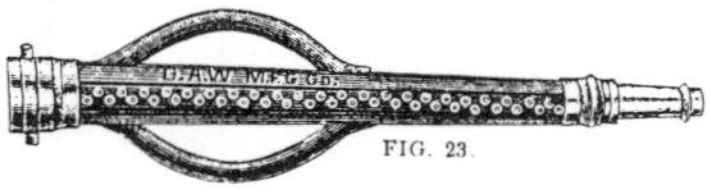

FIG. 23.

2 inch Leather Play Pipes……
2½ " " " ……
2 " " Steamboat Pipes……
2½ " " " ……

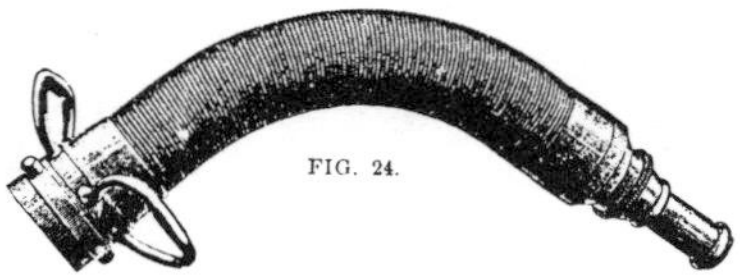

FIG. 24.

2½ inch Callahan Flexible Pipe……

We make any style of Play Pipes with Jones, Gaylord, Fehy, or Universal Connections.

CLEMENS' CONTROLLING NOZZLE.

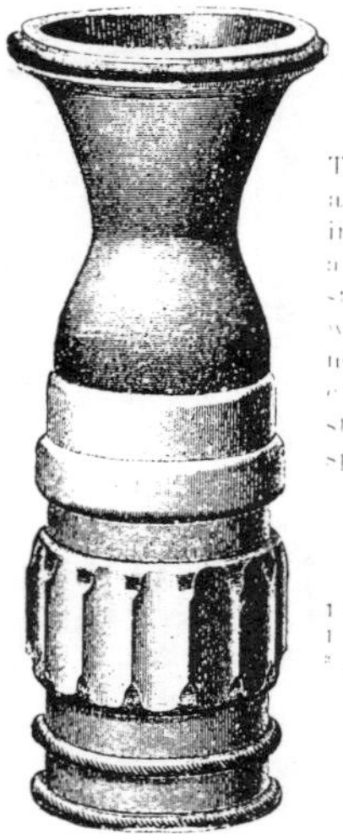

This nozzle throws a stream from 1 1-4 inches to size of an extinguisher stream by the working of its inner cone. Also combines both shut-off and a spray.

1¼ to 1½ size.
1 inch " "
¾ " "

FIG. 30.

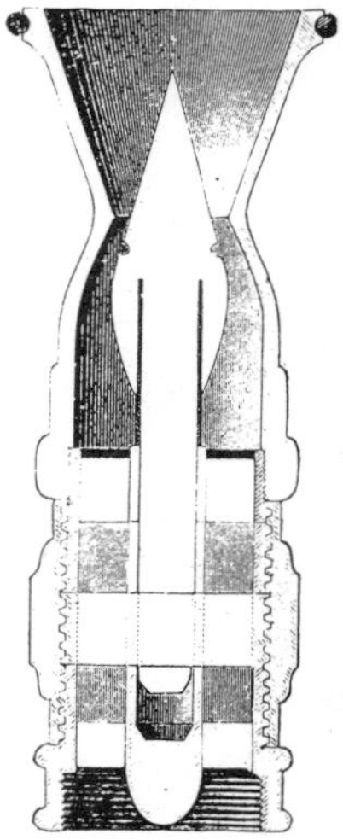

CALLAHAN NOZZLE.

FIG. 31.

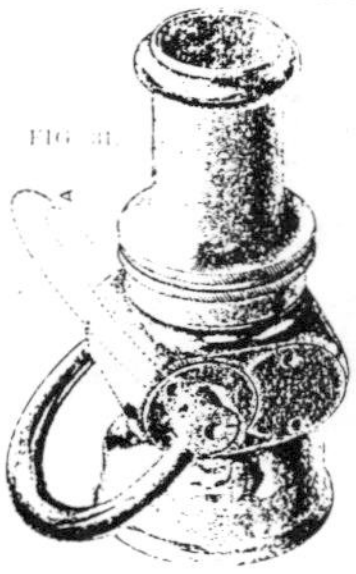

This nozzle has no ground joint and can be taken apart by any fireman with a key which is furnished free. They are made to throw a solid stream or spray, or both combined.

PRICES:

¾ to 1¼ inch, plain
¾ to 1¼ " , plain, with spray
¾ to 1¼ " " " double spray

LARGE SIZES MADE TO ORDER.

Nozzles and Playpipes

Left - 2 1/2" Brass Straight Stream Nozzle
with Leather Handle.
Right - 2 1/2" Combination Nozzle with
Rubber Edged Tip & Leather Handles.

2 1/2" Nozzle with Leather
Wrapped Playpipe and
Handles.

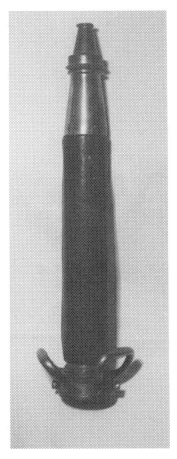

Leather Wrapped
Playpipe & Steamer
Nozzle.

Standard Types of Solid Stream Nozzles.

Nozzles and Playpipes

Left - Underwriters Playpipe, brass with red cord wrapping.
Center - Straight Stream Nozzle with on/off valve.
Right - Straight Stream Nozzle with Rubber Edged Tip.

Selection of Brass Solid Stream Nozzles.

Selection of Different Types of Nozzles.

Nozzles and Playpipes

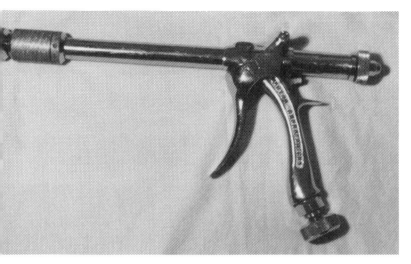

Barton High Pressure Gun, chromium plated, used on a booster line.

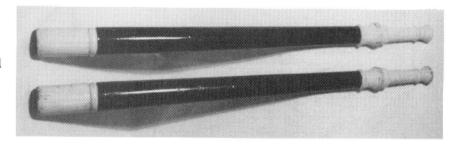

Pair of Wooden Parade Nozzles, painted black & white, early 1900's.

4' Playpipe & Nozzle marked "Here We Are".

Nozzles and Playpipes

PRICE GUIDE FOR NOZZLES AND PLAYPIPES

Brass nozzle, 7" tall, with valve & removable tip, used on chemical engine - $95.00
"Fairy" nozzle, brass, 6" tall with on/off valve - $25.00
11/2" nozzle, brass with valve & rubber tip - $125.00
11/2" combination nozzle, chrome - $65.00
Standard straight stream nozzle, chrome - $20.00
Underwriters playpipe with red cord wrapping, 30" tall - $125.00
4' playpipe & nozzle marked "Here We Are" - $550.00
Leather playpipe & handles with brass nozzle - $350.00
21/2" combination nozzle, chrome with rubber covered handles - $200.00
Pair of wooden parade nozzles, painted black & white - $150.00 pair

Patches

One of the easiest fire collectibles to obtain is the fire department patch. Patches are made in all manners shapes and sizes. Some of the more common shapes are round, shield and maltese cross. Patches are usually n on one or both shoulders of shirts or jackets. Many times a fire department will have a down sized version heir patch made for use on a hat or ball cap.

Years ago patches were sewn by hand. Today, computerized looms stitch flawless, multi-color designs. ny patches currently being produced have a plastic coating on the reverse side to resist wear during washing.

One method of obtaining patches is to write to various fire departments and request their patch. Be sure ndicate your willingness to purchase the patch, as fire departments do incur a modest cost to produce these ns. Many collectors will trade patches for ones they don't have.

PRICE GUIDE FOR PATCHES

Patches - $2.50-15.00

Pedal Cars

One of the hottest areas of fire collectibles is children pedal vehicles in the form of fire trucks and fire chief's cars. Pedal cars have been around since the early 1900's. During the depression of the 1930's, some of the finest examples of pedal fire trucks and chief's cars were made by companies such as American National, Steelcraft and Gendron. Many of these pedal vehicles featured working electric head lights, spot light, horn and siren. In addition, these children's fire trucks had wood ladders, hose reels, upholstered seats and elaborate detailing.

There were also many pedal fire vehicles made in the 50's, 60's and 70's by Murray, AMF and others. These are nice, but not as rare and valuable as pedal cars produced in the 1920's and 1930's.

Pedal Cars

54 Murray City Fire Dept., red with white trim,
wood ladders & bell.

Garton Kidillac Fire Chief's Car, red & white,
1950, note: unusual mounting bracket for bell.

MC Hook & Ladder, red with white trim, wood
ladders, 1950's.

AMF Fire Chief Car #503, 1970's.

Pedal Cars

Garton Fire Truck, red with white trim, wood
ladders & bell, 1949.

AMF Fire Fighter #508, red with yellow
letters, plastic ladders & hubcaps, 1970's.

Murray Champion Fire Chief, white with
red trim, 1950's.

Murray Fire Truck, red with white trim, wood
ladders & bell, 1960, note: battery operated red
beacon on hood.

Pedal Cars

PRICE GUIDE FOR PEDAL CARS

American National, Hose Auto, red & gold with electric lights, fully restored, 1936 - $8000.00-9000.00
Toledo Hook & Ladder, white with green & red trim, 1938 - $2750.00
Skippy Hose Cart, red with white stripes, headlights, rubber hose & siren, 1940 - $4000.00
Steelcraft Airflow Chrysler Fire Truck, 1935 - $3500.00-4000.00
Murray Fire Truck, City Fire Dept., red with white trim, wood ladders & bell, 1954 - $750.00
Murray Fire Truck, red with white trim, with bell & light, 1960 - $250.00-300.00
Murray Champion Fire Chief, white with red trim, 1950's - $300.00-400.00
AMF Fire Chief 503, 1970's - $125.00-175.00
AMF Fire Fighter 508, red with yellow lettering, plastic ladders and hubcaps, 1970's - $125.00-150.00
Garton Kidillac, Fire Chief's Car, red and white with bell - $700.00-800.00
Garton Fire Truck, red with white trim, wood ladders and bell - $850.00-950.00
BMC Hook & Ladder, red with white trim, wood ladders, 1950's - $450.00-550.00

Photographs

Daguerreotype.
These were the first practical photographs invented by Louis Daguerre in 1839. Images were created by the action of iodine and mercury vapors on a silver-coated, copper plate. The image was actually the negative, so images are reversed and cannot be duplicated. Many times the photographs were hand tinted to add color. Most daguerreotypes were small, about 3" x 4" and were placed in a leather or composition case for protection. The surface of the daguerreotype is easily damaged and should not be touched.

Outdoor scenes showing fire apparatus are the rarest because it was difficult to set up equipment outside. Daguerreotypes selected for purchase should be free of excessive amounts of scratches and tarnish. Occupational portraits of firemen in uniform with helmets and trumpets are very desirable.

Ambrotype.
In 1851, Frederick Archer invented the Ambrotype. This process used a glass plate negative with a light sensitive emulsion coating. This negative was mounted over a black backing to display a positive image. The ambrotype didn't reveal as much detail as the daguerreotype. Like dags, ambrotypes were also prone to deterioration and were kept in protective cases. Photographs of firemen are desirable, especially with apparatus.

Tintype.
The tintype or ferrotype was a variation of the ambrotype process. The light sensitive emulsion was coated onto a piece of black or brown, lacquered metal, instead of a glass plate. Tintypes were of a poorer quality than the daquerreotype or the ambrotype. Tintypes were popular during the Civil War and through the turn of the century. Many street photographers continued to use the tintype into the 1930's. Photographs of firemen and apparatus are very collectible. Severely out of focus photographs should be avoided.

Albumen photographs.
The albumen photograph was more prolific and less desirable than the other forms of photographs. These photos were made from wet plate negatives and appear to have a brownish tinge. As with the other types, photos of firemen or apparatus can be used for display or reference material.

Cabinet photographs.
These photographs measured 4" x 5 1/2" and were produced in a studio. Many cabinet photos featured portraits of famous theatrical personalities. Often times a fireman would have his picture taken in this manner.

Carte de visite.
This type of photograph was in the form of a card measuring 4" x 2 1/2", bearing a portrait. Abbreviated CDV, carte de visite means visiting card, or calling card. It was fashionable to exchange CDV's in a similar manner as the modern day business card. Look for cards with portraits of firemen in parade uniforms.

Stereograph cards.
Stereograph cards or stereo cards, are paired photographs placed on a single card. When the card is examined through a viewer, the image appears to be three dimensional. Photographic cards of this nature were popular in the late 1800's. Try to find scenes of great fires, firemen in horse drawn steamers and firemen in uniforms.

Photographic cases.
There are two highly collectible photographic cases with a fire related design. Cases were intended to protect dags, ambrotypes and tintypes. A curious process was employed to make these "thermoplastic" cases. Shellac and dyed wood fibers were heated and this mixture was pressed into dies. The resulting product is known as gutta percha.

One gutta percha case shows a fireman with a helmet and trumpet, leaning on a fire hydrant. Surrounding the fireman is intricate scrollwork. The other case features a design of a fireman descending a staircase, rescuing a child. In the background, firemen operating a hand pumper can be seen.

Photographs

9th Plate Daguerreotype of Fireman Smoking a Cigar, with
original case.

Daguerreotype of Fire-
man Wearing High
Eagle Helmet, 2" x 4".

Tin Type 4" x 5" Fireman in
Parade Uniform.

C.D.V. of Fireman in a Dress Uniform.

Pair of Albumen Photos of Early Motorized Fire Apparatus.

Photographs

PRICE GUIDE FOR PHOTOGRAPHS

Photograph Pricing.
Daguerreotype, Fireman in full uniform, sixth plate, 2¾" x 3¼", 1850's - $950.00
Daguerreotype, Fireman wearing high eagle helmet, sixteenth plate - $800.00
Daguerreotype of a uniformed fireman from Neptune 6 1/6 plate - $1500.00
Daguerreotype, Fireman smoking a cigar with original case, ninth plate - $1200.00
Ambrotype, eighth plate, 2⅛" x 3¼", Fireman in uniform, hand tinted, 1850's - $225.00
Tintype, eighth plate, portrait of a fireman with red shirt, high eagle helmet &
        parade belt, 1860's - $175.00
Tintype, Fireman in parade uniform, half plate - $400.00
Tintype, quarter plate, 3¼" x 4¼", standing fireman in uniform, 1870's - $225.00
Albumen photos of apparatus, firehouses, etc. - $35.00-75.00
Albumen cabinet photos of firemen in uniform - $35.00-75.00
C.D.V. of fireman in a dress uniform - $65.00-95.00
Cabinet photos of firemen - $65.00-100.00
Stereograph cards - $20.00-50.00
Modern photographs - $10.00-50.00

Photographic Cases.
Gutta purcha case, fireman with trumpet leaning on hydrant - $395.00
Gutta purcha case, fireman descending a staircase rescuing a child - $295.00

Daguerreotype of a uniformed fireman from
Neptune 6 1/6 plate.

Plates

Fire collectible plates include original dinnerware used by fire departments as well as collector plates designed by various artists. Many fire departments had their own china. Plates, cups, saucers, pitchers, creamers, etc. can be located with fire department markings. Small sets of dishes with designs are the most desirable to obtain.

Easier to find are colorful collector plates. These ceramic plates had a limited number of firing days. Usually offered for sale through dealers or magazines, these plates feature a variety of fire related themes. Many plates depict early apparatus, fire scenes or dalmatians.

Plates

Collectors Plate 1991 Simon Duplex Pumper.

Collectors Plate with 1908 Steam Fire Engine.

Dish Set Defiance Hose Co. No. #1.

PRICE GUIDE FOR PLATES

Dish set, Defiance Hose Co. - $125.00
Plate with fire department markings - $25.00
Commemorative plate - $35.00-65.00
Collector plates, ceramic - $35.00-95.00

Presentation Shields

Given as gifts of appreciation from one fire company to another, presentation shields were popularly exchanged during the 1800's. Many shields were made of leather and were 8-16" tall. Rare examples were made that exceeded 30" in height. Some shields were made of metal or wood and featured hand painted designs. Artwork could depict flags, famous people, apparatus or a variety of other themes. Raised lettering, inlays, metal ornaments and decorative stitching were typical embellishments of leather shields.

Generally, the larger, more elaborate shields with fine artwork or leathercraft are the most valuable. The collector will find it difficult to locate premium examples of presentation shields as many have been added to museum collections.

Presentation shield, 32" tall, spectacular handpainted & tooled designs on leather. Mutual 1 to Astoria 1. (Restored by a professional artist.)

Presentation shield, 28" tall, tooled and decorated leather with an image of an owl, original paint. Pearl 28 to Liberty Hose 10.

Presentation Shields

Leather Presentation Front.

Left - Leather Presentation Front,
12" tall with hook & ladder design.
Right - Leather Presentation Front,
10 1/2" tall with helmets & hand tub.

PRICE GUIDE FOR PRESENTATION SHIELDS

Leather shield, 16" tall, hand painted - $1500.00-2500.00
Leather shield, 12" tall with hook & ladder design, Empire Hose Co. 1 to Excelsior 1 - $1750.00
Leather shield, 10 1/2" tall with helmets & hand tub, Mohawk 39 to Lexington - $1750.00
Leather shield, 12" tall with metal stag design, Cataract 25 to LaFayette Hose 34 - $2000.00
Large presentation shields - $7500+ rare
Presentation shield "Fairmount 32 Fire Co. Phil. to Perseverance 1 of Bethlehem, PA" - $5500.00
Presentation shield, 32" tall, handpainted & tooled design leather, Mutual 1 to Astoria 1 - $7500.00
Presentation shield, 28" tall, tooled & decorated leather w/image of an owl,
    Pearl 28 to Liberty Hose 10 - $7000.00

Ribbons

Ribbons were produced for various conventions, musters, parades, contests and exhibitions. These ribbons were typically made of silk with decorative stitching. On the ribbon, the sponsor of the event and date can be found. Many ribbons had medals or ornaments attached. Some ribbons had celluloid buttons with pictures of firemen or apparatus as an embellishment.

Ribbons are plentiful, as thousands of examples were generated over the years. Look for large, fancy ribbons with metal ornamentation from the mid 1800's through the turn of the century. A ribbon collection can be nicely displayed by mounting a grouping in a glass frame.

Display of Fire Related Ribbons.

Ribbons

Assortment of Ribbons

Ribbons

PRICE GUIDE FOR RIBBONS

Silk ribbon with sponsors name and date of event - $15.00-18.00
Fancy silk ribbon with ornament attached - $30.00-50.00

Salvage Bags

When a fire occurs, it is not only a fireman's duty to extinguish the flames, but to assist in the salvage of household goods. During the 18th and early 19th century, householders owned salvage bags made of linen. Linen is a cloth made from fibers of the flax plant. Hearing the alarm of fire, householders would throw out their salvage bag along with their fire bucket. Firemen would use this bag to carry valuables from the burning structure. A salvage bag usually had the owners name or initials, and the town name painted on the front of the bag. Once the most common of all colonial items, salvage bags are a rare find today.

Salvage Bags

Linen Salvage Bag, marked "A.B. KELLOGG, GRANBY, 1827".

Linen Salvage Bag, marked "JUDSON HOFF, FRENCHTOWN, NJ".

PRICE GUIDE FOR SALVAGE BAGS

Linen bag with name only - $175.00
Linen bag with name & number - $300.00
Linen bag with name, number, town & date - $425.00

Signs

There are many types of fire collectible signs. Some signs are made of metal such as tin, copper, aluminum or steel. Other signs are made of glass, cardboard, paper, porcelain or wood. Signs were made to identify fire stations, fire chief's offices, fire alarms, fire escapes, fire hose and other insurance signs. Many colorful signs depicted scenes of fire apparatus and other fire related themes.

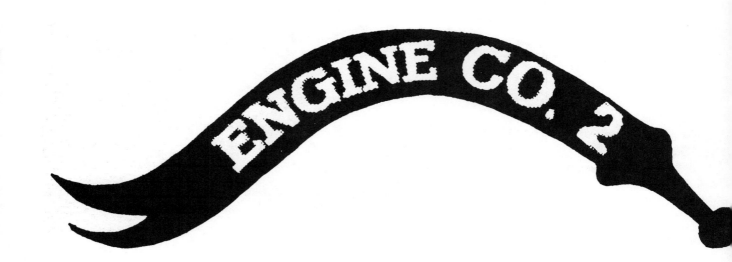

Signs

Fire Insurance Sign, Fireman's Fund Insurance
Company, tin, color, lithography, 36" x 28".

Fire Insurance Sign, Fireman's Fund Insurance
Co., cardboard, 27" x 20 1/2".

Fire Insurance Sign, Fireman's Fund Insurance
Co., cardboard, 27" x 20 1/2".

Fire Insurance Sign, Fire Association, Philadelphia,
reverse painted glass, 25" x 29".

Signs

Fire Escape Sign, tin, red letters and white background.

Tin Signs, painted white with
red letters.

No Parking Fire Route Sign, white
with red letters.

Signs

Fire Equipment Sign, steel, painted red with white letters.

Reproduction Fire Alarm Box Sign.

Fire Alarm Box Sign, tin, painted red & white.

Fire Extinguisher Sign, steel, white letters & red background.

Signs

PRICE GUIDE FOR SIGNS

Wood, Fire Station sign - $200.00-500.00
"Fire Alarm Box", tin - $30.00
Fire "Hose", tin - $25.00
"No Parking Fire Route", steel - $25.00
"Fire Equipment", steel - $30.00
Iron firehouse sign, painted black with white lettering "Engine Co. 2" - $150.00
Fire insurance sign, reverse painted glass, plain - $300.00-750.00
Fire insurance sign, reverse painted glass, w/illustration - $1500.00-3000.00

Smokey Bear Collectibles

In 1945, the Wartime Advertising Council hired Albert Staehle to create a fire prevention symbol. At the time, the Japanese had threatened to set U.S. forests on fire with incendiary ballons. The symbol Mr. Staehle created was Smokey Bear.

In 1950, a burned bear cub was found after a fire in the Lincoln National Forest in New Mexico. It was only logical to name the cub, Smokey. Smokey's fire prevention message, "only you can prevent forest fires" still holds true today.

Many Smokey Bear items were produced over the years. Posters, cards, games , toys and comic books are just a few examples of the types of items that were produced.

Smokey Bear Collectibles

Smokey Bear Toy by
Dakin, vinyl, 1976.

PRICE GUIDE FOR SMOKEY BEAR COLLECTIBLES

Smokey Bear game by Milton Bradley, 1968 - $60.00
Smokey Bear poster, 13" x 18", 1950's - $20.00
Comic book, The True Story of Smokey Bear, 1969 - $20.00
Smokey Bear paper bookmark and ruler - $10.00
Smokey Bear child's leather belt, "Prevent forest fires" stamped on belt with Smokey buckle - $50.00
China salt & pepper shakers, one is Smokey holding a bucket, the other is Smokey
       holding a shovel, 1950's - $40.00
Smokey Bear magnetic cigarette snuffut - $45.00
Smokey Bear vinyl toy by Dakin, 1976 - $35.00
Smokey Bear cover on manual, 1955 - $15.00
Smokey Bear and fire engine on tumbler, 1965 - $20.00

Stamps

One of the least expensive of the fire collectibles is the fire related stamp. There are only five U.S. stamps that can be considered in this catagory. The earliest and most desirable is the three cent, 300th anniversary Volunteer Fireman stamp issued in 1948. The stamp is red in color and features a portrait of Peter Stuyvesant, credited with organizing the first volunteer firemen in 1648. Stuyvesant was the Governor of New Amsterdam and had only one leg. His first band of eight firemen were known as the Prowlers, since they patrolled the streets from nightfall until daybreak.

It wasn't until 1981 before the next fire related stamp would appear. That stamp was the twenty cent fire pumper, a coil stamp considered to be part of the transportation series. This stamp featured an 1860's vintage steam fire engine printed in red with a white background.

The next stamp, a twenty cent Smokey Bear stamp, was issued in 1984. It depicts a frightened bear cub clinging to a burned tree trunk, with the image of Smokey in the background.

In 1988 a 20.5 cent stamp showing a 1913 Ahrens-Fox fire engine was issued. The truck on this stamp is red with a white background.

Christmas 1992 brought a colorful 29 cent stamp with a steam fire engine toy on it. The engine is red with a black and brass accented boiler. "29 USA" is in green with "greetings" printed in red across the bottom.

Since the cost to purchase these stamps is minimal and all are readily available, choose only stamps in mint condition. Place the stamps in clear plastic mount and avoid exposing them to moisture, sunlight or temperature extremes.

0.5¢ Ahrens-Fox Fire Engine, 1988.

3¢ 300th Anniversary Volunteer Fireman, 1948.

20¢ Smokey Bear, 1984.

29¢ Toy Steam Fire Engine, 1992.

20¢ Fire Pumper, 1981.

PRICE GUIDE TO STAMPS

3 cent, 300th Anniversary Volunteer Fireman, 1948 - singles: .20¢   plate block 4: $1.00
20 cent, Fire Pumper, 1981 - singles: .25¢ plate block 4: $1.50
20 cent, Smokey Bear, 1984 - singles: .40¢ plate block 4: $2.00
20.5 cent, Ahrens-Fox Fire Engine, 1988 - singles: .45¢ plate block 4: $2.00
29 cent, Toy Steam Fire Engine, Christmas, 1992 - singles: .45¢

Tools & Equipment

Over the years, firemen have used a variety of unusual tools to accomplish their duty. One such tool used in the late 18th and early 19th centuries was the bed key. These small wrench-like tools were made to unbolt beds. In case of a fire, the beds could be taken out of the home as they were expensive to replace. Bed keys are hard to find and bring high prices.

Another tool frequently used is the spanner wrench. A spanner wrench is used to tighten or loosen spanner caps or hose couplings. Many sizes exist and some varieties of spanners fold up to fit in a coat pocket.

Hydrant wrenches are used to turn fire hydrants on and off. They are very common and their design hasn't changed much over the years.

Pike poles are used to pull down ceilings or poke through walls to check for fire extension. They can also be used to hook objects or for rescue purposes. Look for old wood handle pike poles. These make nice display items since most new pike poles have fiberglass handles.

Many other tools and equipment such as the haligan tool, smoke masks and breathing apparatus, life net, jaws, etc., provide firemen with options to handle various emergency situations.

THROWING A LINE

Tools & Equipment

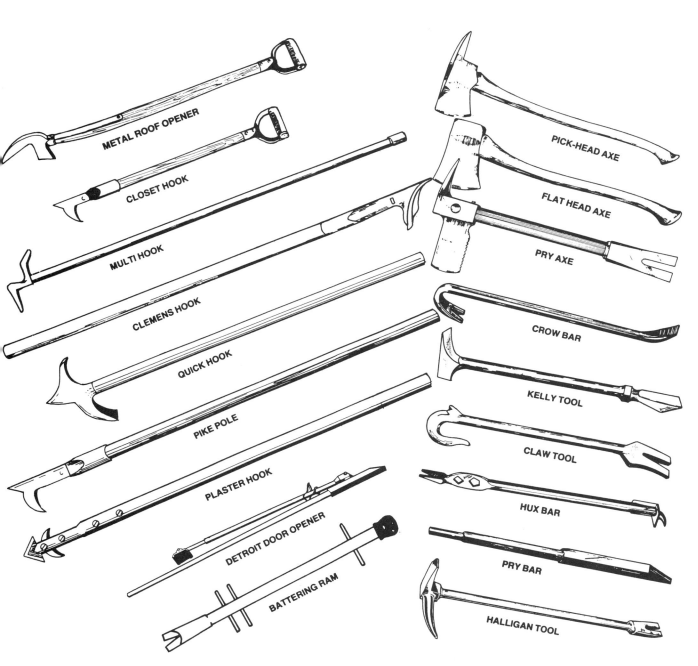

METAL ROOF OPENER

CLOSET HOOK

MULTI HOOK

CLEMENS HOOK

QUICK HOOK

PIKE POLE

PLASTER HOOK

DETROIT DOOR OPENER

BATTERING RAM

PICK-HEAD AXE

FLAT HEAD AXE

PRY AXE

CROW BAR

KELLY TOOL

CLAW TOOL

HUX BAR

PRY BAR

HALLIGAN TOOL

Tools commonly used by firefighters.

Tools & Equipment

SPANNERS OR HOSE WRENCHES.

FIG. 78.

Extra strong Malleable Iron Hose and Hydrant Spanners.

POCKET HOSE SPANNERS.

FIG. 79.
Open.

FIG. 80.
Closed.

Made of Bronze Metal.

Polished . . . .
Nickel . . . .

FIRE HATCHET, BELT AND SHEATH COMBINED.

This cut represents one of our latest improved appliances for Firemen, which is designed to enable Firemen to carry a hatchet with pick for instant use, without running the risk of injuring himself or others by contact with blade or pick.

The sheath has brass end holder for pick and tin-lined end for blade so no injury can occur from contact with hands or body. The lap of sheath is made so same comes over hatchet and buttoned on the outside; thus no liability of hatchet falling out.

Price, complete . . . .

FIG. 81.

EMPIRE LIFE-SAVING NET.

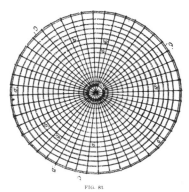

FIG. 83.

CONSTRUCTION OF "NET."

PATENTED MARCH 29, 1887.

TESTIMONIALS.

"Saves Four Lives in New York City."

[Extract from Official Report New York Fire Department.]

March 19th, 6.56 A. M., Station 655, fire was at No. 38 E. 55th Street, S. E. corner Madison Avenue . . . . Foreman Shaw, of that company (13), then ordered the life-saving net spread (the fire in the mean time having cut off all other means of escape, and making it impossible also to raise ladders) and with citizens and firemen holding it, they caught in the net Addie Westlake who jumped from the fifth floor, and Frederick and Isaac C. Westlake, and Assistant Foreman Quirk, who jumped from the fourth floor, by the dense smoke, before any member of the Department could reach her. Mrs. Westlake, the mother of the family, was suffocated to death at the window of the fourth floor, by the dense smoke, before any member of the Department could reach her. Assistant Foreman Quirk, when he jumped landed safely in the net, and afterwards fell out and broke his arm. He, and the three members of the Westlake family, would undoubtly have been killed if it had not been for the life-saving net, as there was no other means of saving them. One of the Westlakes sustained no injury, and the injuries of the other two are from burns received before they jumped, and from shock. . . . .

(Editoral New York "Sun" April 29, 1888.)

Again the fire net worked well at the fire of yesterday morning in West Twenty-eighth Street. It saved the life of one woman, who would certainly been killed if it had not been ready for her. The other women in the upper stories of the house refused to jump into it, but were rescued by other means after receiving injuries which they would not have suffered if they had possessed the assurance needed to take the leap. It seems necessary to repeat, for the information of all who may be imperilled as these persons were yesterday, that the fire net has worked with perfect safety on every occasion in which it has been brought into service in this city. When the fire net is in readiness, any one may without danger spring into it from the fourth, fifth, or sixth story of a burning building.

THIS MAKES 12 LIVES SAVED IN NEW YORK CITY.

DETROIT PATENT DOOR OPENER.

FIG. 157.

This is the best device in use for forcing open store doors, etc., in case fire. With this opener doors can be forced quickly without breaking the gla

EMPIRE LIFE SAVING NET

PATENTED.

This invention relates to improvements in life-saving apparatus for use at fires, and object is to provide a net strong enough to resist the weight of bodies falling from a gr height, and which shall be provided with suitable means about its circumference for ke ing the tension equal. These objects are attained by the mechanism illustrated in the ab cut.

Heretofore appliances used at fires for a similar purpose have consisted either of tex fabric with handles attached around the edge, or else of cotton webbing, in which the w and woof were each in parallel lines and sewed together at the points of crossing. Th forms of apparatus were not sufficiently strong to resist the weight of falling bodies were liable to sag. By means of this invention these difficulties are entirely removed.

Made of the best Russian hemp, which guarantees strength. At the same time construction of the apparatus is such that it may be rolled up and packed in a very s space. The net is ten feet in diameter and weighs 35 pounds.

This lightness and compactness adapt them for the equipment of any Hook and La Truck, Hose Wagon, Carriage or Patrol Wagon.

Adopted by the Fire Departments of New York, Brooklyn, Cleveland, O., New Ha Ct., Baltimore, Md., Bayonne, N. J.

Tools & Equipment

panners or Hose Wrenches.

FIG. 73.

panner, 2½ in. $12.00 a dozen. | Steel Spanner, 2 in.

Patent Spanner.

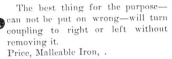

FIG. 74.

The best thing for the purpose—can not be put on wrong—will turn coupling to right or left without removing it.

Price, Malleable Iron, .

Taber's Spanner.

Will turn the Coupling to right or left without removing it.

Malleable Iron, Galvanized, ...

FIG. 75.

Fire Hook.

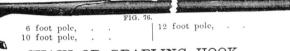

FIG. 76.

6 foot pole,   .   . | 12 foot pole,   .   .
10 foot pole,   .   .

CHAIN OR GRAPLING HOOK.

arge size, with chain and pole, ...

CROW BARS.

FIG. 72.

x 55 inches, painted . . . .
x 55   "   polished. . . . .
x 55   "   "   and plated . . . .

FIRE DEPARTMENT SUPPLIES.

HURD'S
Patent Respirator
or
Smoke Protector.

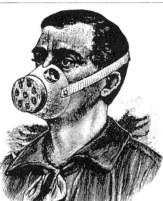

Designed to enable a person to enter or pass through a building filled with smoke.

In respiring, the air is inhaled through a wet sponge or cotton, and in expiring passes out through a valve in the side.   Made of pure white rubber.

Spanners or Hose Wrenches.

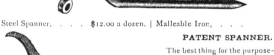

Steel Spanner,   .   .   . $12.00 a dozen. | Malleable Iron,   .   .   .

PATENT SPANNER.

The best thing for the purpose—cannot be put on wrong—will turn coupling to right or left without removing it.

Price, Malleable Iron,

Taber's Spanner.

Will turn the Coupling to right or left without removing it

Price, Malleable Iron, Galvanized, ...

Fire Hook.

6 foot pole,   .   . | 12 foot pole,   .   .
10 foot pole,

CHAIN OR GRAPLING HOOK.

Large size, with chain and pole, ...

Tools & Equipment

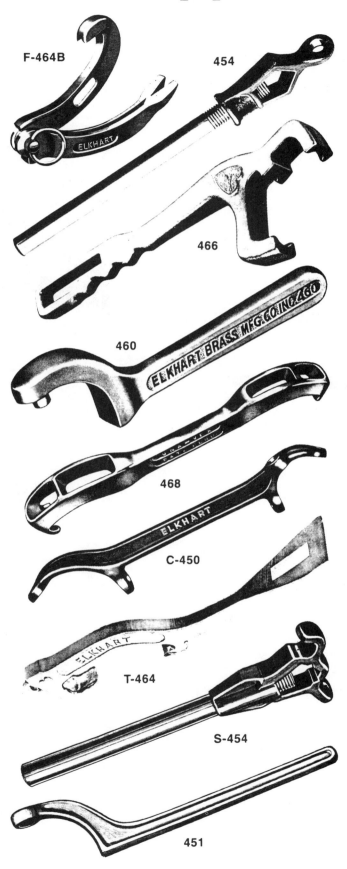

F-464B

454

466

460

468

C-450

T-464

S-454

451

Selection of Spanner & Hydrant Wrenches.
Original Catalog Page

Tools & Equipment

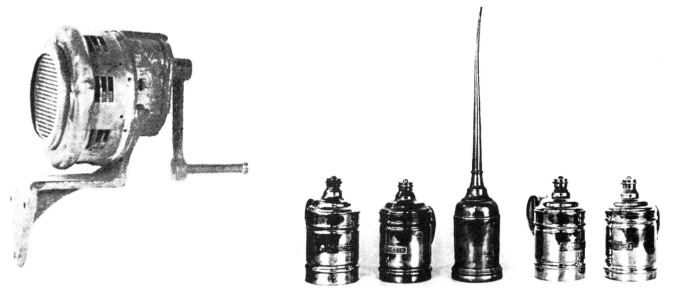

Hand Crank Siren.

Brass Oil Cans for lubricating steam fire engines.

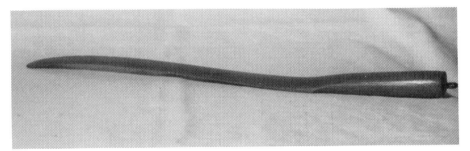

Sweat Stick made of wood, used to remove
the lather from hot fire horses.

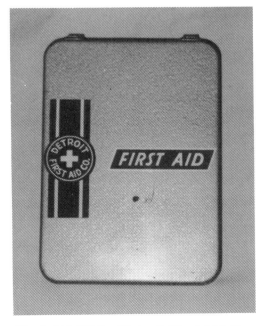

First Aid Kit by Detroit First Aid Co.

Bed Key or Wrench, used to unbolt
beds from burning houses, cast
iron.

Tools & Equipment

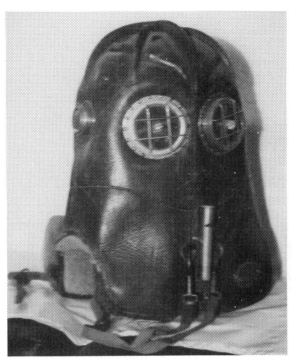

Front View of the Vajen Head Protector, Vajen Bader Co., Richmond, IN, used by Manistee, MI Fire Dept., 1900.

Rear View of the Vajen Head Protector, Vajen Bader Co., Richmond, IN, used by Manistee, MI Fire Dept., 1900.

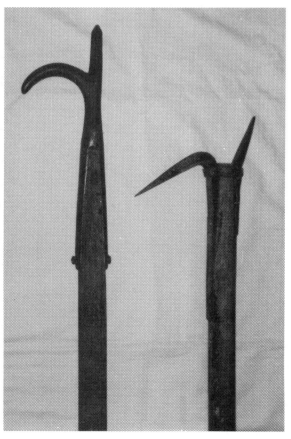

2 Types of Pike Poles with wood handles, 1930's.

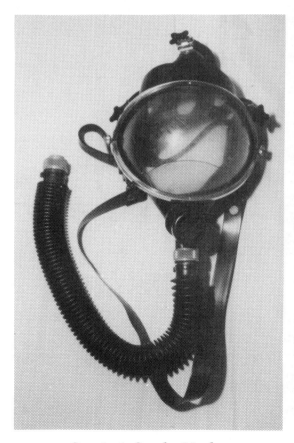

Survivair Smoke Mask.

Tools & Equipment

Guages from Old Fire Apparatus.

Three Element Rotating Warning Light,
red lenses, Buckeye Roto-Rays.

Combination Red and Clear Spotlight
with Twist Grip Control.

Brass Searchlight, 18" diameter.

Tools & Equipment

PRICE GUIDE FOR TOOLS & EQUIPMENT

Bed key, cast iron - $175.00
Spanner wrench - $15.00
Pike pole, wood handle - $50.00
Vajen Head Protector, 1900 - $300.00
Survivair smoke mask - $25.00
Fire coat, 1940's - $50.00
Fire boots, rubber - $20.00 pair
Red beacon, 8" diameter, 1950's - $65.00
Rotary light, 3-element - $295.00
Spotlight, brass, 18" diameter - $495.00
Lifenet - $500.00
Detroit door opener - $65.00
Pry bar - $20.00
Halligan tool - $65.00-75.00
Sweat stick, wood-used on fire horses - $40.00
Hand crank siren - $400.00
Brass oil can used to lubricate steam fire engines, marked American Fire Engine Co. - $550.00-650.00
Pressure gauge from an old steamer - $55.00
Spotlight, red & clear with twist grip control - $65.00
Rope throwing gun - $1500.00-1750.00
First aid kit, Detroit First Aid Co. - $35.00
Compound gauge from a fireboat. American LaFrance Fire Engine Co. - $75.00

Compound gauge from a fireboat.
American LaFrance Fire Engine Co.

Torches

Torches were used to light the way to a night fire and were carried by junior members of the company known as torch boys. Parades were another event in which torches were used. Groups of firemen marching with lit torches must have been quite a spectacle for the townsfolk.

Most torches were affixed to a handle or pole and were carried. Specialized torches were placed atop helmets or caps in order to leave the fireman with his hands free.

The stationary torch was designed to be mounted on the apparatus and could be removed and placed on the ground.

Typically, a torch had a wick and a reservoir of some type. Fuel that was burned in the torch could be coal oil, whale oil or tallow. Certain torches had screw-on wick caps, wick picks or were designed to use candles. Cone-shaped flambeaus made of tin were also used.

Fire department markings can authenticate a torch used by the fire service. Torches were also used in political campaigns and by the military. Look for polished brass or silver torches with turned wooden poles. Double swing torches made of tin are fairly common and less valuable. However, these torches make nice display items. Stationary torches are sought after by apparatus restorers as well as fire antique collectors. Unusually shaped torches, such as torches in the shape of a viking style fire axe, are extremely rare and valuable.

Torches

DOUBLE SWING TORCH.

FIG. 58.

Quarts, polished brass,   nickel plated,

Pints,   "   "   "   "

HOSE CART TORCH.

FIG. 59.

Polished brass, with cap and chain,   ·nickel plated,

ENGINEER'S HAND TORCH.

FIG. 60.

Copper,   polished,   nickel plated,

Torches

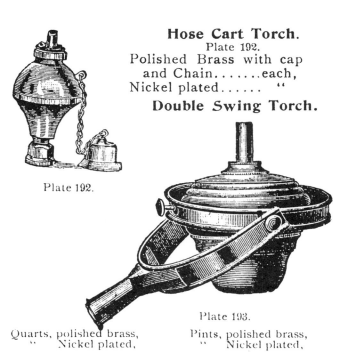

Hose Cart Torch.
Plate 192.
Polished Brass with cap
and Chain......each,
Nickel plated...... "

Double Swing Torch.

Plate 192.

Quarts, polished brass,
"   Nickel plated,

Plate 193.

Pints, polished brass,
"   Nickel plated,

Helmet Torches.
Plate 194.
For parade purposes ;
made of heavy spun brass.
Easily attached to helmet.

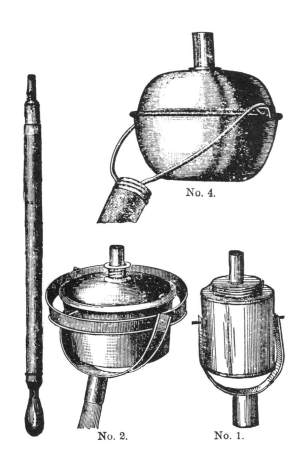

No. 4.

No. 2.   No. 1.

Plate 194.

Engineers' Hand Torch.

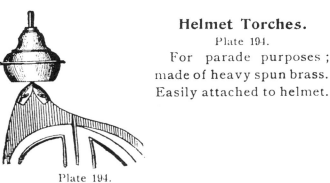

Plate 195.

Polished Brass........   Nickel Plated.. .....

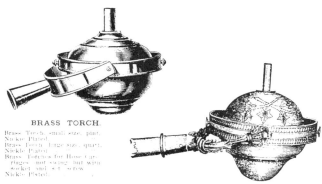

BRASS TORCH.
Brass Torch, small size, pint,
Nickle Plated.
Brass Torch, large size, quart,
Nickle Plated.
Brass Torches for Hose Car-
riages, not swing, but with
socket and set screw.
Nickle Plated.

New Design Silver Plated Fancy Torch.

Torches

Brass Torch, 6" diameter, missing handle.

Parade or Dress Cap with Torch.

Fancy Silver Plated Parade Torch with medallion of a fireman with torch, 37" long.

Brass Hose Cart Torch, whale oil, marked Seagrave, 1870's.

Brass Hose Cart Torch with Cap & Chain.

Torches

Selection of Tin Torches with wood handles.

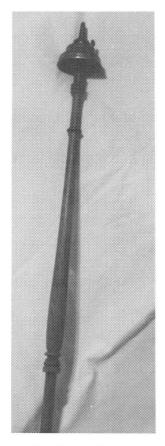

Torch used on a chemical engine, brass with turned oak pole.

Wood Parade Torch, painted black, 1870's.

Plain Tin Double Swing Torch with handle.

Torches

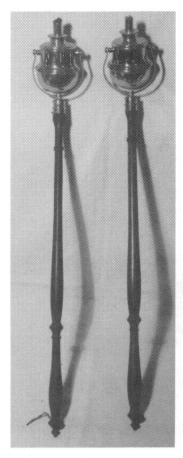

Pair of Parade Torches, polished brass, double swing torches with nicely turned hardwood handles.

Pair of Tin Parade Torches with wood handles.

Pole Lamp, tin with eagle finial, "#1 Brigade, Brooklyn, New York".

Torches

PRICE GUIDE FOR TORCHES

Polished brass, double swing torches, with nicely turned hardwood handles - $395.00 pair
Plain tin, double swing torch with wood handle - $75.00
Tin, wood handle, used on a chemical engine - $150.00
Brass, whale oil torch marked Seagrave, circa 1870's - $250.00
Tin, wood handle painted black, parade torch, circa 1870's - $200.00
Brass torch, double swing with large spherical reservoir, missing handle - $135.00
Parade cap with torch - $225.00
Parade torch shaped like a viking style fire axe - $1450.00
Parade torch, silverplated with medallion of a fireman with torch, 37" long - $1500.00
Parade torch, polished brass with carved wood handle, marked "Tompkins Company". - $2500.00

Parade torch, polished brass with
carved wood handle,
marked "Tompkins Company".

Toys, Candy Containers & Molds

Toys

Prior to the 1880's, few firefighting toys were commercially produced. Early toy hand pumpers, hose carts and hose reels were made of wood and tin. Many of these toys were handmade, one of a kind items.

Around 1890, cast iron fire apparatus toys such as horse drawn steamers, hook & ladders, hose wagons, fire patrol wagons and Fire Chief's wagons were produced by various toy manufacturers. Generally, these cast iron toys were colorfully painted and featured rolling wheels, removable cast iron firemen, ladders or hose.

In addition, most toy apparatus of this era had one, two or three cast iron horses hitched to the apparatus. Many times the horses were attached by a lever to a wheel. When the toy was pulled along the floor the wheel and lever would move. This would cause the horses to travel up and down, making them appear to gallop.

Famous toy makers of this era includes: Pratt and Letchworth, Ives, Carpenter, Hubley and Wilkins.

By the early 1900's through the 1920's, horse drawn toys disappeared and motorized fire apparatus toys emerged. Self propelled steamers, hook & ladders and water towers with wind up motors were produced by Hubley and Kingsbury toys.

The roaring twenties and the following depression years brought a multitude of collectible firefighting toys. Large pressed steel fire trucks by Buddy L, Keystone, Sruditoy, Steelcraft and Marx were popular then and are highly desirable today. Many of these toys had working lights, bells, ladders or pumps and could actually squirt water. A large number of pressed steel toys were over three feet long and some were designed for a small child to ride on.

During this time, Hubley produced a great number of cast iron, toy fire trucks. A great percentage of these toys had nickel plated parts and white rubber wheels.

Cast iron fire trucks were not the only toys being produced. Cardboard fire hats were made with decorative helmet fronts. Games and puzzles with fire engines were also popular during this time and have become collectible.

The advent of World War II created a shortage of metal. However, a few toy manufacturers such as Tootsietoy and Dinky continued producing small, cast-metal fire engines. The Auburn Rubber Company produced a molded rubber fire engine in two different styles.

The 1950's brought more steel fire trucks from Marx, Doepke, Buddy L, Hubley, Structo and Tonka. In the area of small, die cast toys, Lesney began producing its famous "Matchbox" cars and trucks. Plastic was becoming the fastest growing new material for toys. The Texaco Fire Chief helmet is an example of a collectible plastic toy.

During the 1960's, Japanese tin toys were sold all across the United States. Many examples were rather fanciful and featured friction or battery operated mechanisms. Fire Chief's cars, ladder trucks, snorkels, fire boats and jeeps were made by a variety of toy manufacturers. Taiyo, Yonezawa, Ichiko, Nomura and Bandai were a few of the Japanese toy makers. Later tin toys produced in Taiwan are not as desirable as Japanese tin toys.

Hot Wheels produced an ambulance and a two piece fire truck as part of its "Heavyweights" series. Matchbox produced several fire chief's cars, fire trucks and ambulances during this period.

Another collectible item from the 1960's is a tin "Emergency" lunch box, based on the popular TV series of the same name. Two versions of this lunch box exist. One is dome shaped and the other is the standard, rectangular box. Look for examples complete with the thermos.

Collectors of toy fire trucks from the 70's, 80's and 90's look for quality and fine detail. A great number of these toys are constructed of metal and plastic. Conrad, Corgi, Solido and Hess are just a few of the many producers of fire truck toys. Toys related to the movie "Backdraft" such as plastic model kits and toy helmets are certainly destined to become future collectibles.

Serious toy collectors try to obtain premium condition toys in the original box. Other collectors are happy with toys that can be displayed and handled by their children. Demand, availability, age and condition determine a toy's value. Certain toys have incalculable sentimental value to their owners. A father or grandfather may have played with a particular toy as a child and gave that toy to his child or grandchild.

Reproduction toys are frequently offered for sale, especially cast iron fire apparatus. Generally, reproductions have a rough casting and fresh paint. However, some unscrupulous individuals have attempted to age these reproductions to look like originals. Check with a reputable dealer if there is any question regarding authenticity.

Naturally, broken or incomplete toys are less desirable. There are reproduction parts such as wheels, tires, ladders, etc. available to repair many fire apparatus toys. As with other firefighting collectibles, toys in excellent original condition are preferred over restored examples.

Toys, Candy Containers & Molds

Candy Containers & Molds

During the 1920's, novelty glass candy containers in the shape of motorized steam fire engines were sold. In many instances, they were filled with multi-colored beads of sugar. The bottom of the container was sealed with a paper label. When a child had finished the candy, the container could be used as a toy. These containers were used through the 1940's until it was realized that giving small children glass toys was unsafe. If one is found, examine it closely for cracks and chips.

Chocolate molds and ice cream molds were also made in the shape of steamers. Lead was used for the chocolate molds and pewter for the ice cream molds. Many of these items are being reproduced, so shop carefully.

Another collectible candy container is a plastic PEZ dispenser with a fireman's head figure. PEZ is short for pfefferminz, the German word for peppermint. In 1952, PEZ candy was introduced to the U.S. The PEZ fireman has a black handlebar mustache and a red fire hat.

Toy motorized steamer.
Cast iron, Made by
A.C. Williams Co., circa 1920s.

Toy motorized steamer, pressed steel
with aluminum wheels. Brass bell and
rails. Nickel-plated boiler. Made by
Buddy L., 231/4" long, circa 1890s.

Toy horse drawn fire patrol wagon,
cast iron. Features opening tool chest
under rear step and galloping
motion when pulled. 203/4" long,
made by Ives, circa 1890s.

Toy hose reel cart, cast iron,
galloping motion when pulled, made
by Carpenter, circa 1890s.

Toy ladder truck, removable nickel-
plated ladders and driver. Made by
Hubley. 131/2" long, circa 1940s.

Toy high eagle helmet with
decorated front piece.

Toys, Candy Containers & Molds

Early Toy Hand Tub, 12" long, dated 1822.

Climbing Firemen Toys.

Reproduction Cast Iron Motorized Steamer.

Kenton Steam Fire Engine, 1920's.

Cast Iron Arcade Pumper, 1930's, known as the "Six Man Blue", missing bell between middle two firemen.

Toys, Candy Containers & Molds

Marx Hook & Ladder Truck, pressed steel.

Puzzle showing children
rescuing a cat from an
alarm box, 1940s

Buddy L Fire Truck.

Tonka Aerial Ladder Truck.

Keystone, chemical pump engine,
pressed steel.

Buddy L Aerial Ladder Truck, red, pressed steel,
39" long, 1920's.

Toys, Candy Containers & Molds

Keystone Aerial Ladder Truck, 31" long, pressed steel, 1920's.

Sturditoy Water Tower Truck, 32" long, pressed steel, 192

Hubley Cast Metal Fire Ladder Truck, 1930's.

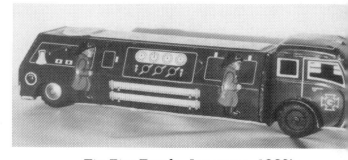

Tin Fire Truck, Japanese, 1960's.

Toys, Candy Containers & Molds

Hubley Cast Metal Fire Engine, 1930's.

Pressed Tin Fire Jeep, made from a beer can, Occupied
Japan, 3" long.

Tin Fire Chief's Car, Japanese, friction drive, 1960's.

Marx Fire Station with Chief's Car, pressed tin, 1950's.

Toys, Candy Containers & Molds

Wind-up Tin Fire Truck, 2 /2" long, 1960's.

Stamped Tin Fire Chief's Car, 2" long.

Marx Pressed Tin Ladder Truck, 1950's.

Plastic Open Cab Fire Truck, wind-up mot
1960's.

Auburn Pumper, made of rubber, painted red & silver, WWII era.

Tin Wind-up Fire Chief's Car, by Co
land Mfg. Co., early 1950's.

Toys, Candy Containers & Molds

Midgetoy Fire Chief's Car, 3 1/4" long, cast metal, 1950's.

Matchbox Fire Chief Car, Superfast Series, die cast, 3" long, 1976.

Wheels Fire Chief Cruiser, by Mattel, die cast, red line tires, 3"
long, 1968.

Matchbox Mercury Fire Chief's Car, Superfast Series, die cast, 3"
long, 1970.

Toys, Candy Containers & Molds

Matchbox Fire Chief Ford Galaxie, by Lesney, die cast, 2 3/4" long.

Toy Fire Badge, tin, made in Japan, modern.

Toy Fire Badge "Junior Fire Marshal - Hartford Fire Insurance Co.", red plastic, pin back.

Toy "Fire Men" Badge, tin, Japanese, 1950's.

Fire Chief Bicycle Siren, tin, 1950's.

Fire Chief Paper Noise-maker.

Toys, Candy Containers & Molds

Texaco Fire Chief Helmet with Advertising Display,
Parks Plastics Co., 1950's.

Emergency Dome Top Lunch Box,
1960's.

Rectangular Style Emergency
Lunch Box.

Fireman Nutcraker,
painted wood.

Future Fire Collectible Toy,
Teenage Mutant Ninja Turtles
"Hose 'Em Down Don", by
Playmates.

Toys, Candy Containers & Molds

Left - Glass Candy Container, Motorized Steam Fire Engine.
Center - PEZ Fireman, plastic.
Right - Glass Candy Container, Ladder Truck.

Small Glass Candy Container with original paint, 5" long, 2" tall.

Fire Space Patrol tin,
made in Japan, circa 1960s.

Ice Cream Mold, Fireman
with Trumpet, pewter,
5 1/2" tall.

Toys, Candy Containers & Molds

PRICE GUIDE FOR TOYS, CANDY CONTAINERS & MOLDS

Cast Iron Toy Pricing.
Ives Firehouse with clock work motor & horse
    drawn steam fire engine, 1890's - $5000.00+
Ives Fire Patrol Wagon, 1890's - $1950.00
Ives Hook & Ladder, 1880's - $1500.00
Wilkins Hose Cart, 1890's - $450.00
Wilkins Hook & Ladder, 1890's - $1200.00
Wilkins Steam Fire Engine, 1910 - $1200.00
Kenton Hook & Ladder, 1920's - $1000.00
Kenton Pumper, 1920's - $1400.00
Kingsbury Pumper, 1920's - $400.00
Kingsbury Hook & Ladder, 1920's - $450.00
Hubley Water Tower, 1920's - $1200.00
Hubley Hook & Ladder, 1920's - $1750.00
Hubley Pumper, Ahrens-fox, 1930's - $3950.00
Hubley Pumper, 1930's - $700.00
Hubley Hook & Ladder, 1930's - $600.00
Carpenter Steam Fire Engine, 1880's - $1500.00
Carpenter Hook & Ladder, 1880's - $1200.00
Pratt and Letchworth Steam Fire Engine,
    1880's - $2000.00
Arcade Pumper, "Six Man Blue", 1930's - $600.00
Toy horse reel cart, by Carpenter - $1250.00
Toy horse drawn fire patrol wagon by Ives - $1850.00
Toy motorized steamer by AC Williams - $350.00

Pressed Steel Toy Pricing.
Buddy L Aerial Ladder Truck, 1920's - $1200.00
Buddy L Pumper, 1930's - $1000.00
Kingsbury Steam Pumper, 1930's - $2200.00
Kingsbury Aerial Ladder, 1930's - $2200.00
Helmet Big Boy Fire Truck, 1920's - $2200.00
Helmet Aerial Ladder, 1920's - $2200.00
Sturditoy Water Tower, 1920's - $1500.00
Sturditoy Pumper, 1920's - $1500.00
Keystone Water Tower, 1920's - $950.00
Keystone Aerial Ladder, 1920's - $950.00
Steelcraft Hook & Ladder, 1920's - $1250.00
Marx Ride-on Fire truck, 1940's - $250.00
Structo Pumper, 1950's - $175.00
Structo Aerial Ladder, 1950's - $195.00
Tonka Pumper, 1950's - $225.00
Tonka Aerial Ladder, 1950's - $225.00
Texaco Fire Chief Pumper by AMF Wren-Mac,
    1950's - $275.00
Keystone chemical pump engine - $1500.00
Toy motorized steamer by Buddy L - $2500.00

Tin Toy Pricing.
Marx Fire Chief car, 1950's - $45.00
Marx Fire Station, 1950's - $125.00
Japanese tin Fire Chief's car, 1960's - $50.00-100.00
Japanese tin Fire truck, 1960's - $75.00-125.00
Tin, Fire Chief bicycle siren, 1950's - $25.00

Emergency lunch box, rectangular type, 1960's - $65.00
Emergency lunch box, dome top, 1960's
    w/thermos - $175.00
Disney Firefighters lunch box, 1950's,
    dome top - $125.00
Fire Space Patrol tin, Japan, circa 1960s - $95.00

Miscellaneous Toys Pricing.
Auburn Pumper, rubber, 1940's - $40.00
Texaco Fire Chief Helmet - $65.00
Tootsietoy Fire truck, 1940's - $35.00
Hot Wheels Fire Chief, red line tires - $25.00
Matchbox by Lesney, Fire Chief's car,
    Ford Galaxie - $40.00
Conrad L.T.I. Ladder Tower truck, cast metal,
    1980's - $125.00
Hess Pumper, 1970's - $125.00
Corgi Airport Crash Tender, 1970's - $85.00
Pressed Tin Fire Jeep, Occupied Japan, 3" long - $18.00
Wind-up Tin Fire Truck, 2 1/2" long, 1960's - $15.00
Dinky MerryWeather Marquis Fire Tender,
    1960's - $85.00
Climbing Fireman, tin - $225.00
Paper Noisemaker, Fire Chief - $7.50
Toy high eagle helmet - $100.00
Toy ladder truck by Hubley, circa 1940s - $250.00

Games Pricing.
"Going to the Fire", made by Milton Bradley,
    1920's - $195.00
"Fighting the Flames", made by Sam'l Gabriel,
    1920's - $275.00
"Fearless Fireman", made by Hassenfeld Bros. - $95.00
"Fire Fighters!", made by Saalfield Publishing Co.,
    1957 - $40.00
"Game of Fire Department", by Milton Bradley,
    1930 - $85.00
"Fire Alarm Game", by Parker Bros., 1899 - $2000.00+
Jigsaw puzzle, 20 pc. red fire truck by Milton
    Bradley, 1950's - $30.00
Toy badge, tin, 1950's - $20.00
Toy badge, Junior Fire Marshal, Hartford Ins. - $15.00
Puzzle showing childred rescuing a cat - $35.00

Candy Container Pricing.
Motorized Steam Fire Engine, clear glass,
    small - $35.00
Motorized Steam Fire Engine, clear glass, large - $60.00
PEZ Fireman - $75.00

Molds Pricing.
Ice Cream Mold, pewter fireman - $150.00
Ice Cream Mold, pewter fire engine - $150.00
Chocolate Candy Mold, lead fireman - $195.00
Chocolate Candy Mold, lead steam fire engine - $195.00

Trophies

Firefighters have traditionally been very competitive. To quench this competitive thirst, fire companies departments have participated in an uncountable number of musters, contests, parades, exhibitions, and spo events. For the winners or honored heroes there was often a trophy presented. Trophies can be found in a va of configurations from small loving cups to large ornately decorated tankards and pitchers. These trophie normally silver plated, or on rare occasions, solid silver or gold plated. Many trophies featured miniature exam of firefighters equipment as an embellishment.

Generally, the more ornate and unusual the trophy, the greater its value. Many times the silver plat be worn or flaking on a trophy. It is possible to have the item replated. Be sure the plater will not harm inscription or engraving on the trophy.

Trophies

Trophy Pitcher, silver plated with hinged lid.

Silver Plated Loving Cups, dated 1923, 1916 and 1933, these trophies were awarded to different fire companies for various events.

Trophies

PRICE GUIDE FOR TROPHIES

Loving cup, silver plated, 6" tall with sponsor's name and date of event - $75.00
Loving cup, silver plated, 10" tall with sponsor's name and date of event - $100.00
Pitcher, silver plated with hinged lid, 12" tall with decorative engravings - $150.00
Large ornate, solid silver trophy, lavishly decorated with miniature firefighting
     equipment - $2500.00-3500.00
Small ornate, solid silver trophy with miniature firefighting equipment - $650.00-1500.00
Pair of silver plated goblets by Rogers & Smith - $8000.00 pair
Fire company bowling trophy, 1915 - $1500.00

Pair of silver-plated goblets, 15" tall, by Rogers and Smith. The lids feature a fireman in full dress with fire hat and cape holding a long nozzle. Wonderful engravings of a hose cart, surrounded by wreaths and scrolls, adorn these goblets.

Fire company bowling trophy with highly detailed etching of an old time bowling alley and participants. "Morristown Fireman's Bowling League, Y.M.C.A. Alleys, 1915, won by Humane Engine Company. In original gilt frame with black border.

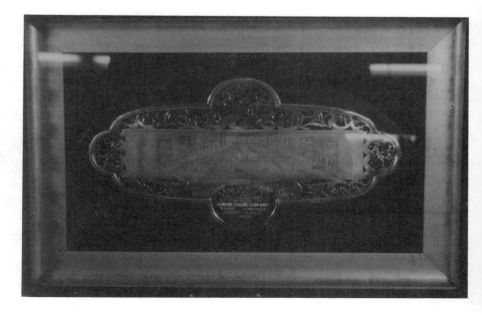

Trumpets

Communication between firefighters today is just as important as it was in the 1800's. During that era, the speaking trumpet or horn, became very popular as a means to direct the sound of the human voice. A foreman could use his trumpet to shout orders to his men, or to sound the alarm of fire. These types of trumpets are known as working trumpets or duty trumpets. If a fight broke out at the fire, as when rival fire companies met, the trumpet could be used as a bludgeon. When the fire was out and it was time for celebration, the trumpet could be brought to the local tavern. Here, the men would remove the mouthpieces from their trumpets, plug the bottoms and fill them with ale. However, this use of the trumpet was not universal as many towns had strict laws forbidding the consumption of alcohol.

In addition, trumpets were presented as gifts. For example; when an honored chief retired, or from one fire company to another for assisting at a large fire. These types of trumpets are known as presentation trumpets or parade horns. When in a parade, the recipient of such a gift trumpet carried a bouquet of flowers in the bell.

Trumpets were made in a variety of shapes and sizes. Essentially they consist of four parts; the mouthpiece, the tube, the tassel mounts, and the flared bell. Metals generally used in the construction were solid brass, nickel plate or tole (painted tin) for working trumpets and silver plate or solid silver for presentation trumpets. A small percentage of trumpets were made of copper, glass, leather, or hard coal. Certain specially created and highly rare trumpets had gold inlaid designs, gold plating and were laden with semi-precious stones. Trumpets with unusual tassel mounts such as dolphins, eagles or fire helmets are much sought after.

When considering a trumpet for your collection, examine it carefully. Severely dented trumpets or ones with missing parts such as the mouthpiece or tassel mounts are far less desirable than complete specimens. Often the silver plating has deteriorated on many presentation trumpets. This shouldn't discourage the collector from acquiring the trumpet, as the piece can be replated. If you decide to have a trumpet replated, make sure the plater can preserve any delicate engraving. Remember a dedicated trumpet is perferred over a non-dedicated one. Finally, check to see if the trumpet has the original tassel. Reproduction tassels are available and do not detract too greatly from the value of a nice trumpet.

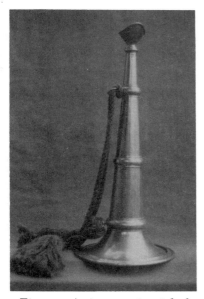

Fireman's trumpet, nickel plated brass with tassel.

Presentation trumpet, silver plated with floral engravings and scalloped bell. Replacement tassel.

Eight-sided fireman's trumpet, pewter with replacement tassel.

Trumpets

Presentation and Parade Trumpets.

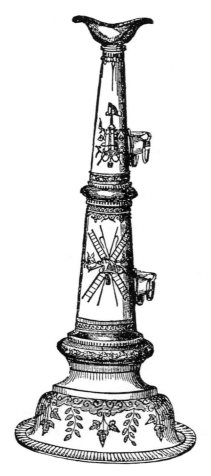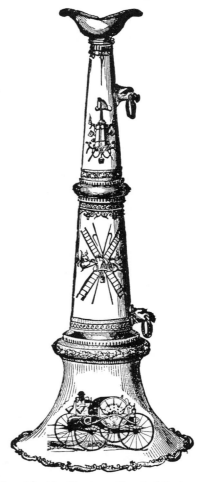

Engraved with Steamer, Hand Engine, Hose Carriage, Hook and Ladder Truck, or Chemical Engine

16 inch, chased and plated, ...
18 " " " . . . . . .
20 " " " . . . . . .
16 " extra chased and plated, bell and mouth-piece gold-lined, .
18 " " " " " " "
20 " " " " " " " "
22 " " " " " " " "
20 " extra handsome, emblems in relief, finished in best style, extra heavy
plated, gold-lined bell and mouth-piece, and silver cord and tassel,

Cord and Tassels (for Trumpets.)

Cotton, ...
Silk, ...
Silver, ...

Trumpets

FIREMEN'S TRUMPETS.
Duty Trumpets.
Plate 291.

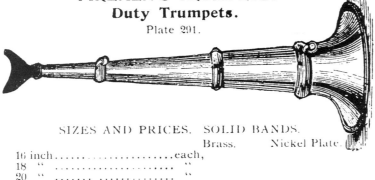

SIZES AND PRICES. SOLID BANDS.

	Brass.	Nickel Plate.
16 inch......................each,		
18 " .... "		
20 " .... "		

Strap Handles.
With snap hooks for trumpets..................each,

Parade and Presentation Trumpets.
Plate 292.

HEAVILY SILVER PLATED.

No. 3, 19 inches high, gold lined...............each,
No. 4, 20   "   "   " .... "

Plate 293.

WITH SCALLOPED AND FLUTED BELL.
GOLD LINED.

No. 4, 22 inch, satin engraved.......................
No. 4, 22   "   embossed and chased.................

Cords and Tassels.
Red or blue.....................................each,

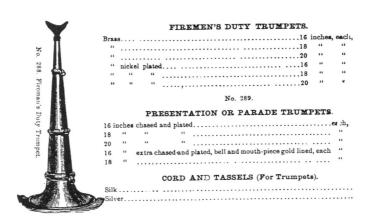

No. 288. Fireman's Duty Trumpet.

FIREMEN'S DUTY TRUMPETS.

Brass...	16 inches, each,	
"	18 "	"
"	20 "	"
" nickel plated..........................	16 "	"
" " "	18 "	"
" " "	20 "	"

No. 289.

PRESENTATION OR PARADE TRUMPETS.

16 inches chased and plated...................................	each,
18 " " "	"
20 " " "	"
16 " extra chased and plated, bell and mouth-piece gold lined, each	"
18 "	"

CORD AND TASSELS (For Trumpets).

Silk ....
Silver...

Original Catalog Pages

Trumpets

TRUMPETS.

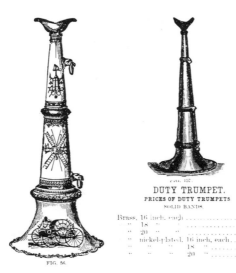

FIG. 56.

FIG. 157.

DUTY TRUMPET.
PRICES OF DUTY TRUMPETS
SOLID BANDS.

Brass, 16 inch, each . . . .
" 18 " " . . . .
" 20 " " . . . .
" nickel-plated, 16 inch, each, .
" " " 18 " " . . .
" " " 20 " " . . .

PARADE TRUMPETS.

PRESENTATION OR PARADE TRUMPETS.

16 inch, Chased and Plated . . . .
48 " " " . . . .
20 " " " . . . .
16 " " " Bell and mouth-piece gold lined . . . .
18 " " " " " " " . . . .
20 " " " " " " " . . . .
22 " " " " " " " . . . .
22 and 25 inch, extra handsome, extra heavy plated, best style . . .
   Steamer, Hand Engine, Truck or Hose Carriage, chased on Parade Trumpets to order at a small additional cost. Names and Letters engraved on Trumpets at low figures.

TRUMPETS

FOR PRESENTATION PRIZES, CONTESTS, ETC.

Nos. 345, 346 and 347 are made of white metal, triple silver plated, the bell and mouth piece are gold lined. All the ornamentations are richly engraved and chased.

——————

We present our standard styles which are usually kept in stock for prompt delivery. When engraving is desired, allow us time to make up to order.

——————

Price for engraving inscription on application.

Style No. 346 shown in color on page 27.

No. 347
Silver Plated, Gold Lined,
22 inches high

FIREMAN'S TRUMPETS.

No. 124.   No. 125.   No. 126.

PATENT OCTAGON TRUMPET.—No. 124.

   The shaft is made octagon, or eight sided, and the bell a pleasing combination of circle and angle. It is decidedly the handsomest trumpet made, and has proved a great favorite.
   They are made with solid bands, and are finished in brass or nickel-plate. Suitable for duty or parade.

Brass, 2 bands, 16 inches, . . . | Nickel Plated, 2 bands, 16 inches,
" 3 " 18 " . . . | " 3 " 18

PATENT OCTAGON PARADE TRUMPET.—No. 125.
Full finished, with gold plated mouth and bell.

18 inch, ... | Without gold plating, . . .

ROUND DUTY TRUMPET.—No. 126.

Brass, 16 inch . . . . . . | Nickel Plated, 16 inch, ...
" 18 " . . . . . . | " 18 " . . . .
" 20 " . . . . . . | " 20 " . . . .

CORDS AND TASSELS FOR TRUMPETS.

Worsted, for service trumpets, ... | Silk, for presentation trumpets.
Silk, for parade trumpets.
   These cords and tassels are made in a variety of plain colors including the different shades of red, blue, green, dark yellow, etc.; also in combination of these colors.

No. 346

FANCY TRUMPET

Silver Plated—Gold Lined Mouth and Bell, 19" high. Price . . . .

Extra for red or blue silk cord and tassels . . . .

Trumpets

Duty Trumpets.

MILLER'S
"Corrugated" Bell and "Solid Band"
FIRE TRUMPET.
The Best Duty Trumpet Made.

Trumpets made on the old plan of **hollow bands** and **plain bell**, become bruised after having been in use but a short time, to repair which requires the trumpet to be taken apart, but when made with **Corrugated Bell and Solid Bands** will outlast three of the old style and look handsome while in use.

This Trumpet is not only the strongest but the handsomest one now offered to the Fireman.

PRICES.

14 inch, Brass,		14 inch, Nickel Plated,
16 " "		16 " " "
18 " "		18 " " "
20 " "		20 " " "

Old style Trumpet, plain bell and hollow bands, furnished at 10 per cent. discount from above prices.

Patented May 18, 1875.

MILLER'S
CORRUGATED FIRE TRUMPET

Can be had of all dealers in Fire Department Supplies.

It is endorsed by all firemen who have used it, and they are now in use in nearly all the principal Fire Departments in the United States, Canada and South America.

This Trumpet furnished with ornamental work to suit any purpose, with apparatus engraved on the bell suitable for Steam Fire Engine, Hand Engine, Hook and Ladder, Hose, or Chemical Engine Companies—shield in front with raised representations of the apparatus used in the fire department.

Extra Chased.

16 inch	. . . .
18 "	. . . .
20 "	. . . .
22 "	. . . .

Extra Chased.

WITH GOLD-LINED BELL AND MOUTH PIECE.

16 inch	. . . .
18 "	. . . .
20 "	. . . .
22 "	. . . .

Extra Handsome.

EMBLEMS IN RELIEF, FINISHED IN BEST STYLE, EXTRA HEAVY PLATED, GOLD LINED BELL AND MOUTH PIECE, AND SILVER CORD AND TASSEL.

| 20 inch | . . . . |

Presentation and Parade Trumpets.

Always on hand, ready for immediate delivery, a large assortment of all Sizes and Styles.

Of Solid Silver and Silver Plated, of any size or shape, with appropriate designs handsomely engraved or chased on them, suitable for any occasion. Trumpets for tournaments and fairs. When parties desire it, three or four trumpets will be sent to select from.

THE LATEST DESIGN OF PARADE TRUMPET.

ORNAMENTATIONS ARE ALL IN RELIEF.

18 inch, fully ornamented,	. . . .
20 " " "	
18 " " "	gilt bell and mouth-piece, ...
20 " " "	"

TRUMPETS

For prizes or presentations we have a variety of designs in trumpets which are suitable for the purpose. These trumpets vary in size and finish.

Style No. 92 shows a plain Trumpet furnished in polished brass or nickel. When trimmed with silk cord and tassels it makes a very creditable appearance and will serve the purpose very well in case funds are not available for the more beautiful and costly silver Trumpet styles No. 345, No. 346, No. 347.

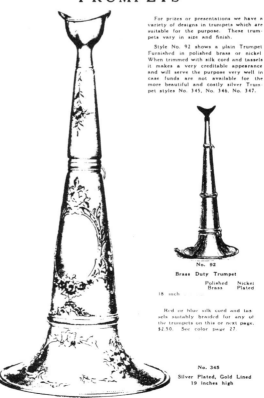

No. 92

Brass Duty Trumpet

Polished   Nickel
Brass   Plated

18 inch

Red or blue silk cord and tassels suitably braided for any of the trumpets on this or next page. $2.50. See color page 27.

No. 345

Silver Plated, Gold Lined
19 inches high

Trumpets

Presentation Trumpet, repoussé with neptune, 21" tall, 1854.

Presentation Trumpet, silver plated, 18" tall, 1880, note: unusual firemen's helmet tassle holders.

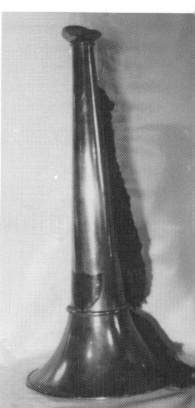

Presentation Trumpet, brass 18" tall, 1858.

Cranberry Glass Fire Trumpet with clear crossbanding and leaf pattern, extremely rare.

Trumpets

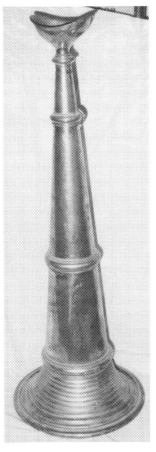

Miller's Corrugated
Fire Trumpet,
1880's.

Fabulous presentation
trumpet. Repousse floral
patterns, polished brass,
22" tall.

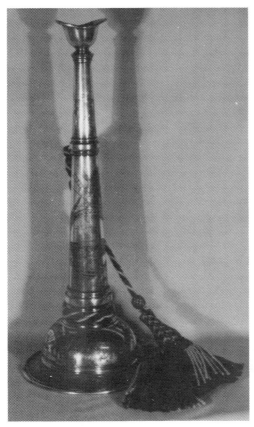

Presentation Trumpet, silver plated,
21" tall.

Presentation Trumpet, sterling
silver with exquisite floral
repoussé, Neptune Steam Fire
Co., 20" tall, 1867.

Trumpets

Presentation Trumpet with unusually wide mouthpiece.

Presentation Trumpet, silver plated, 21" tall, note: eagle tassle holders.

Unusual presentation trumpet, with early hydrant, and twisted riveted hose. Engraved floral motif on bell, silver

Working Trumpet, made of tole, pre-civil war era.

Trumpets

PRICE GUIDE FOR TRUMPETS

Presentation Trumpet, with early hydrant, and twisted riveted hose, engraved floral
   motif on bell, silver-plated - $7000.00
Presentation Trumpet, silver plated with floral engraving and scalloped bell - $1500.00
Presentation Trumpet, repousse floral patterns, polished brass, 22" tall - $8000.00
Presentation Trumpet, silver plated with helmet tassle holders (no inscription) – $1150.00
Presentation Trumpet, silver plated, 21" tall, repousse with figure of Neptune, 1854 - $3750.00
Presentation Trumpet, brass, 18" tall, 1858 - $900.00
Presentation Trumpet, sterling silver with exquisite floral repousse, 20" tall,
   Neptune Steam Fire Co., 1867 - $3500.00
Presentation Trumpet, silver plated, 18" tall with firemen's helmet tassle holders, 1880 - $2500.00
Miller's Corrugated Fire Trumpet, 1880's - $675.00
Presentation Trumpet, silver plated, unusually wide mouthpiece - $950.00
Presentation Trumpet, silver plated, 21" tall with eagle tassle mounts - $1750.00
Working Trumpet, made of tole, Pre-Civil War era - $425.00
Brass Working Trumpet, 17" tall - $650.00
Reproduction Brass Working Trumpet - $95.00
Cranberry Glass Trumpet with clear crossbanding & leaf pattern - $15,500.00
Eight sided firemans trumpet, pewter - $950.00
Fireman's trumpet, nickel plated brass - $750.00

Presentation Trumpet, silver plated with helmet tassle holders (no inscription).

Uniforms

In the early 1800's there was no standard style of uniform for firemen. Many firemen wore stovepipe hats, capes or drab overcoats with armbands. About 1850, New York firemen began wearing red shirts, blue trousers with a leather belt, and high leather boots. Suspenders or galluses with the company name or number were also commonly worn. Soon, single and double breasted shirts with the number or first letter of the fire company became popular. These "bibbed" shirts with decorative buttons could be ordered in a variety of colors.

Firemen that were on housewatch at the fire station wore a neckerchief which was secured with a neckerchief ring. Many neckerchief rings were shield-shaped, nickel plated, and had a company number attached.

The finest appearing fireman's uniform was and still is, the parade or dress uniform. Parade uniforms could include a fancy, double breasted coat, vest, parade helmet or dress cap, fancy leather belt, white gloves, and even a bow tie.

Although expensive, the ideal way to collect a uniform is to obtain a complete uniform. In this manner, all the items will match. However, the collector should not be discouraged from acquiring fine examples of individual uniform items as these items are quickly disappearing.

Fireman's bib shirt, red wool
with applied #1.

Uniform cap with
brass badge.

Uniforms

UNIFORMS

No. 501
Frock Coat

The outfit pictured above, helmet, frock coat uniform, white gloves and neat leather belt, makes a highly dignified showing. The coat is regularly made with six pairs of buttons on the breast.

SHIRTS.

FIG. 104. (No. 1.)   FIG. 105. (No. 2.)

FIG. 106. (No. 3.)

No. 1 is the plain Shirt made of F. and C. Flannel, any color.

No. 2, made of F. and C. Flannel, any color trimmed around collar, breast and cuffs, including monogram.

No. 3.—This Shirt is made to button to the neck. The lapels are arranged to be thrown open as in cut, displaying a different color from the Shirt, or to be worn closed, presenting the appearance of a plain Shirt.

RUBBER GOODS.

Rubber Coat, Snap Fastenings.

A superior article in Rubber Coats, made expressly for Fire Service.

They are on drill, double coated, dull finished in black, with improved snap fastenings, which are vastly superior to buttons. They have also straps at throat and wrist.

FIG. 89.

Rubber Caps.

Skull Cap, with full cape opening in front for face.

Rubber Buckets.

Rubber body with rubber handles.

Lettering 10 cents per letter.

Rubber Gloves.

Suitable for Pipemen. They are all made large, and calculated to be worn over another glove.

White or black, sizes 1, 2 and 3.

regular . . . .
with gauntlets . . . .

HANNAFORD

FIG. 90.

VENTILATED RUBBER BOOT . . . .

Ordinary Rubber Boots.

No. 1 . . . .
"   2 . . . .
"   3 . . . .

No. 1.   No. 2.

No. 3.   No. 4.

No. 1.—Double-breasted, plain, red or blue flannel.
No. 2.—Same as No. 1, with initial or No. on breast.
No. 3.—With shield on breast, collars and cuffs trimmed, and two letters or monogram on breast.
No. 4.—Same as No. 3, but with monogram on breast.

The highest priced Shirts are made of the best twilled flannel.

Firemen's Regulation and Parade Shirts.

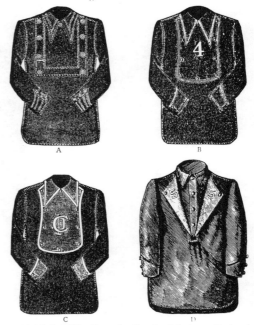

A   B

C   D

Made in Red, White, Blue or Gray Flannel, and also in a combination of colors, with band or cord trimmings, and either Nickel or Gilt Fire Department Buttons. Send for prices and samples of Flannel.

Uniforms

Fireman's Parade Cuffs, leather with felt shield
& silver buttons.

Leather Shield with Brass
Numerals, worn on galluses
to identify the fire company
that a fireman belonged to,
1850's.

Neckerchief Ring
used by a fireman
on housewatch.

Bibbed Fireman's Shirt, blue flannel with gold trim &
buttons, note: galluses or suspenders.

Uniforms

Parade Helmet, Dress Cap and Leather Belt from Montgomery, PA, these items are modern and were custom made for the department.

Pair of vintage fireman's boots.

Fireman's Dress Uniform Coat with Fancy Buttons.

Neckerchief & leather slide with applied #1

Uniforms

PRICE GUIDE FOR UNIFORMS

Frock Coat – $265.00
Complete uniform of Montgomery 1, high eagle helmet, parade belt,
     shirt, cap & pants (modern) - $750.00
Fireman's flannel bibbed shirt with company number, decorative trim & buttons - $200.00
Fireman's uniform cap, dark blue cloth with black visor - $35.00-75.00
Neckerchief ring, shield shaped, nickel plated with company number - $150.00
Galluses with company number - $135.00
Leather shield worn on galluses - $85.00
Matched set, bibbed shirt, dress cap & parade belt - $575.00
Fireman's dress uniform coat with fancy buttons - $80.00
Fireman's bib shirt, red wool with applied #1 - $200.00
Uniform cap with brass badge - $75.00
Neckerchief & leather slide with applied #1 - $150.00
Pair of vintage fireman's boots - $50.00-75.00

Turn of the Century Frock Coat. Wool,
camel color with navy accents and F.D. buttons.

Warden's Staffs

In the early 1700's, Fire Wardens were appointed to take charge at fires. Fire Wardens would direct citizens in forming bucket brigades. They could also enforce fire laws, levy fines, and arrest looters. In order to easily recognize a Fire Warden, it was mandated that he carry a five foot long wooden staff, painted red, with a flame-like brass spire. This staff was a symbol of authority and was only issued to a select group of leading citizens. The staff also came in handy to shove or prod unruly members of the crowd at a fire. Wardens staffs are very rare and valuable with most specimens installed in museum collections. There is another type of wooden staff that has a round knob instead of a spire. Unless these staffs have fire company markings on them, there is no way to guarantee these aren't just ordinary walking sticks.

Warden's Staffs

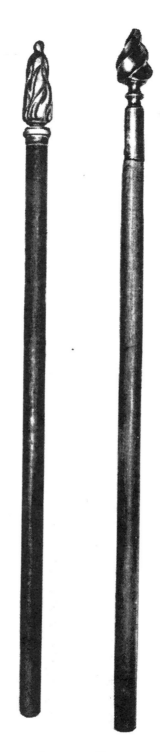

Warden's Staffs, wood
handles with flame-like
brass spire.

PRICE GUIDE FOR WARDEN'S STAFFS

Extremely Rare - $3000.00-5500.00

Watches & Watch Fobs & Clocks

Watches were made in Germany as early as the 1500's by Peter Henlein. In America, watches began to be produced in 1750. However, it wasn't until the 1880's when factories produced watches which made them affordable to the public.

Pocket watches had their heyday in the late 1800's and early 1900's. Many of these watches had elaborate engravings, jeweled movements and cases made of silver or gold. A great number of firemen owned pocket watches. Often a gold pocket watch was given as a gift to a retiring fireman.

Watch cases could be made of solid gold in 18K, 14K, 10K, or 8K. Solid gold watches are rare as most gold pocket watches were actually gold-filled. Gold filled cases were made by sandwiching a layer of base metal between two layers of 10K or 14K gold. Silver or Silveroid was also used for watch cases. Silveroid was a compound of nickel, copper, and manganese.

Very desirable are watch cases with damascening. Damascening is a process of inlaying ornate designs in metal with precious metals.

U.S. watchmakers included: Elgin, Waltham, Hampden, Howard, Columbus, Hamilton, and Seth Thomas among others.

The perfect accessory to any pocket watch is a watch fob. A watch fob is a short chain, ribbon, or leather strap attached to a pocket watch and worn hanging in front of the vest or waist. In many instances, an ornament or seal was affixed to the fob. Many watch fobs were advertising give-aways from apparatus manufacturers. Watch fobs are still being produced, so know what you are buying.

Steamer wall clock
electric with flickering light.

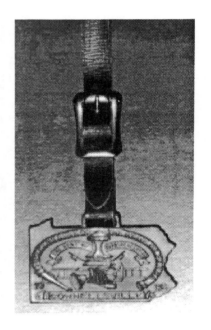

Watch FOB – Brass with Leather
Strap. From Fireman's Assoc. of
Cunnellsville, PA, dated 1935.

PRICE GUIDE FOR WATCHES & WATCH FOBS & CLOCKS

Watch FOB, Firman's Assoc. of Cunnellsville, PA – $45.00
Solid gold presentation pocket watch - $750.00-1500.00
Silver presentation pocket watch - $500.00-1000.00
Waltham watch, NYFD Chief on face, leather band - $325.00
Watch fob with apparatus, original - $75.00
Reproduction watch fob - $10.00-20.00
Steamer wall clock electric with flickering light - $45.00
Watch fob, 1922 convention - $35.00
Watch fob, New York Fireman's Assoc., 1936 - $70.00
Watch fob, Franklin Fire Insurance, brass, bust of Benjamin Franklin, fire pumper - $60.00

Watchman's Rattles

During the 1800's, a town watchman would patrol the streets at night ever on the alert for the first signs of a fire. Upon discovery of a fire the watchman would sound the alarm by spinning a wooden rattle or ratchet. Naturally, the watchman would sound a verbal warning of "fire". However, the rattle provided that extra level of noise as the clacking sound penetrated the stillness of the night.

Rattles were typically made of wood such as mahogany, oak, or maple. They featured a turned handle with a cog, a reed, and a weighted end. As the rattle is spun, the reed drags across the cog and makes a loud "clacking" noise. The weighted end provides momentum to help keep the rattle spinning. Rattles can have single or double reeds. Some rattles have brass weights and folding handles.

Generally a more unusually designed rattle with double reeds or elaborately turned handles, will command the highest price. Not all rattles were used exclusively for fire alarms. Many were used by the police and the military for security purposes. There was even a rattle made as late as WWII to sound a gas attack.

When purchasing a rattle, try spinning it to check its operation. Note if there are any chips or splits in the wood and if the reed has been replaced. Be sure to include a watchman's rattle in your collection as they can be very amusing to show.

Motion Lamp

Motion lamp with forest fire scene
in vivid red, orange and yellows.
Cast metal base and top.
$175.00

Watchman's Rattles

Single Reed Watchman's Rattle, version without brass weighted end.

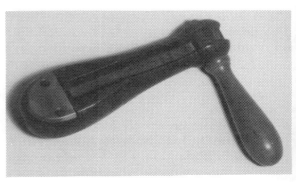

Single Reed Watchman's Rattle, wood with brass weighted end.

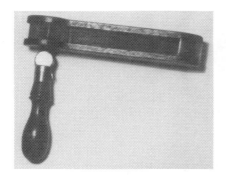

Single Reed Watchman's Rattle, wood with brass weight and folding handle.

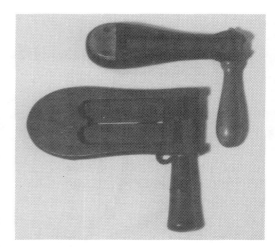

Single and Double Reed Watchman's Rattles.

PRICE GUIDE FOR WATCHMAN'S RATTLES

Single reed, wood rattle with brass weight - $125.00
Double reed, wood rattle with brass weight - $150.00
Wood rattle with folding handle - $175.00
Single reed, wood rattle with crank handle - $185.00

Weathervanes

It was customary during the 19th century to include a finely crafted weathervane on top of a newly built firehouse. Weathervanes were typically constructed of copper, bronze, or zinc, and were available in a variety of motifs.

The Fiske Company produced a catalog in 1893 of weathervanes. Some of the weathervanes designed for firehouses included a fireman's trumpet with helmet, a hook and ladder design, a steam fire engine, and a fireman figure climbing a ladder with a trumpet in hand. These weathervanes were created by true craftsmen and were very expensive to produce. Sizes were made to order with a 7 foot-long model of a steam fire engine available for $275.00.

Today, original examples of firehouse weathervanes are rare as not many were made. Many examples have sold recently for thousands of dollars. Current styles of fire related weathervanes and reproductions are available at a fraction of the cost of an original.

Fireman's Hat & Trumpet Weather-vane.

Firehouse weathervane, maker unknown, trumpet and axe.

Weathervanes

Fireman Climbing Ladder Weathervane, full-bodied copper, 38" tall with 5' arrow.

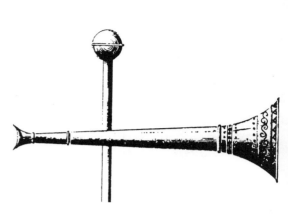

Fireman's Trumpet Weathervane, 33" long.

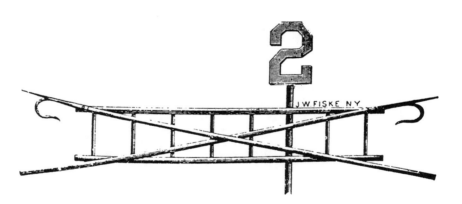

Hook & Ladder Weathervane, 6' or 7' lengths.

PRICE GUIDE FOR WEATHERVANES

Rare fireman's trumpet weathervane - $15,000.00-20,000.00
Rare fireman's hat & trumpet weathervane - $30,000.00-35,000.00
Rare hook & ladder weathervane - $30,000.00-35,000.00
Extremely Rare fireman weathervane, fireman climbing ladder with trumpet
     & five foot arrow - $50,000.00+
Firehouse weathervane, maker unknown, trumpet and axe - $1500.00

A Public Service Message

Please do your part to prevent needless injury or loss of life in a fire.

Think and act in a safe manner.

Install smoke detectors on every level of your home.

Change the batteries in your smoke detector twice a year.

Keep a fire extinguisher handy.

Don't leave food cooking unattended.

Never use gasoline as a cleaner.

Have an escape plan and practice it with your family.

Learn First Aid and CPR.

Support your local fire department.

Notes

Date Purchased	Item	Price	Purchased From:	Date Sold:	Sold

Notes

te Purchased	Item	Price	Purchased From:	Date Sold:	Sold To: